Business Knowledge for IT in Investment Management

A complete handbook for IT Professionals

UK Edition

Essvale Corporation Limited
The Forward Thinking Company

PROFESSIONAL SERIES

Essvale Corporation Limited
63 Apollo Building
1 Newton Place
London E14 3TS
www.essvale.com

This is the first edition of this publication.

Essvale Corporation Ltd is hereby identified as author
of this work in accordance with Section 77 of the
Copyright, Designs and Patents Act 1988

Requests to the authors should be addressed to:
permissions@essvale.com.

A CIP record for this book is available from the British Library

ISBN (10-digit) 0955412412
ISBN (13-digit) 978-0955412417

This publication is designed to provide accurate and authoritative
information about the subject matter. The author makes no representation,
express or implied, with regard to the accuracy of the information
contained in the publication and cannot accept any responsibility or
liability for any errors or omissions that it may contain.

Cover design by Essvale Design Team
Design and typesetting by Boldface, London EC1
Printed by Lightning Source Ltd, Milton Keynes

Preface

This is the second publication for the Business Knowledge for IT Professionals series that will include other exciting topics in the near future. This book focuses on the Investment Management industry in the UK. Investment Management in the context of this book encompasses Asset Management, Fund Management and Money Management.

This publication covers topics including an overview of investment management, the major players, types of funds under management and key business processes. Also covered are trends in the investment industry and the common systems used in the industry. After reading this publication, readers will have the confidence to talk to the business users within investment management, knowing that they have a firm grasp of what the business is all about.

The types of IT professional that would benefit from the knowledge in this publication include software developers, development managers, test analysts and managers already working in investment banking or those that might want to pursue a career in this industry. Other types are project managers, database administrators, support analysts and business analysts that are already working in investment management or would like to cross over from other industries.

Undergraduates, post-graduates and those who have recently graduated can also benefit greatly from reading this publication.

Readers who feel that they would need instructor-led classes to support the knowledge gained from this manual should log on to **www.essvale.com** to browse the relevant courses and to register their details. In addition, we are going to launch a service to support this training initiative and the Bizle Professional Series publications on **www.bizle.biz** so readers are advised to check the Essvale website regularly to get details of when the service will be fully operational.

Finally, readers should please note that some of the data published is not up to date. This is as a result of our limitations in accessing data in some market segments such as hedge funds. The data in this publication is meant to be a guideline to the state of the markets and not a basis for extrapolation or forecasting.

Acknowledgements

Essvale Corporation Limited would like to thank all authors and publishers of all materials used in compiling this publication. Also thanks to all the respondents to the research carried out to justify writing this publication.

We would like to acknowledge Lizzie Margerison of Staspro, Shahla Haque and Nicole Beauregard of Charles River Development, Melanie Smith of Latent Zero, Pete Hudson and Beth Stansby of Linedata, Toby Winn of DSTi, Alistair Turner of Sparx, Michael Harriman of Positive View, Nik Bienkowski of ETF Securities, and Paul Dunay of Bearings Point. Also Mark Robertson of Eiris, Selina Staines of the Investment Management Association, Paul Satar of Ernst and Young, Ian Hunt and Troy Travlos of Investment Horizon, William Jooste and Paul Miller of Morse.

Our thanks also go to Andrew Hilton of Infoline, Claudio Olivier of efinancial news, Magda Covino of DataMonitor, Mike Ross of Tabb Group, Gary Owen of SwissRisk, Byron Baldwin of Deutsche Börse, and Olivier Renault of Citigroup. We appreciate the time you have taken to respond to our requests.

We would not wish to forget to acknowledge Pat Winfield of Bookworm Editorial Services, Barney Lodge of Lodge Consulting, Chris Skinner of Balatro, Stuart Fitzgerald of Kingston Business School, Professor Mike Holcombe of Sheffield University, Professor Anthony Finkelstein of University College London, the helpful staff of City Business Library and Idea Store Canary Wharf, the editors and support staff at Nielsen Book Data, Daniel Page and Sara Fisher of Lightning Source, Duncan James of Wiley Finance, Vic Daniels of Hereisthecity.com, Maggie Berry of Women-in-Computers, Steve Miller of Singapore Management University, Helen Boddy of the British Computer Society, the press officers and CIOs of global investment banks, the staff of Amazon and other bookstores worldwide. Thanks for supporting Bizle Professional Series thus far.

Contents

Introduction

Information Technology has become increasingly integrated with business success. Indeed, the leverage of IT has provided the strategic competitive advantage and differentiation required to sustain organisations in almost every industry sector. Organisations that grasp the concept of attracting, developing and retaining staff who can combine a knowledge of business needs, precedence and competitive differentiation with a sound understanding of IT and connection to business have a competitive edge over their rivals.

In the investment management industry, and in fact any industry, getting the best out of IT professionals requires redesign and implementation of strategies to ensure that they are knowledgeable about the business and a critical component of the overall long-term business strategies. IT is no longer about systems and technology; it is about people and processes.

Why is business knowledge of investment management important?
IT professionals need to have knowledge of the investment management industry for the following reasons:

- Investment management firms need high-quality systems to ensure the smooth operation of the business.
- Business-critical IT projects in investment management firms are executed to very aggressive deadlines and hence there is little provision for training IT professionals in the rudiments of the business justifications and implications of these projects.
- Errors in the output from IT systems can lead to fines from regulators.
- The future of IT demands that professionals have the specific industry knowledge to implement and support business-critical systems.
- The trends in the IT industry are changing the profession into a more specialised than generalised profession.
- Purely technical roles are increasingly outsourced to developing countries where labour costs are more competitive.
- To foster greater understanding between IT and the business with the benefit of creating more harmonised, multi-disciplinary project teams that will compress project timelines.

The benefits of an IT career in investment management are enormous. Permanently employed IT professionals in investment management can earn an average of 15%[1] more than their counterparts in other financial services companies and up to 20% more than in other industries. Contractors, on the other hand, can earn up to 40–50% more than their counterparts in other industries, depending on the area of investment management they specialise in.

1   Estimate based on the outcome of independent research.

Furthermore, investment management firms use the latest and most advanced relevant technology in their operations, so the relevantly skilled IT professional can be ahead of the pack in terms of technical ability.

A career in investment management also offers other benefits as follows:

- The opportunity to move from one firm to another as the business practices are almost identical.
- The opportunity to work in various locations across the world as some of the projects are part of global initiatives.
- The advantage of the location of the investment banks; they are usually centrally located in the West End, the City or Canary Wharf in London.
- The concentration of firms in these locations makes movement between them relatively easy.

The topics discussed in this publication were carefully selected to ensure a wide coverage of the theoretical underpinnings of the investment management discipline as well as to demonstrate the alignment with IT. Business processes and tasks in the day-to-day activities of investment management are mirrored in the associated business processes in IT systems, hence the necessity for the IT professional to have a firm grasp of these activities.

This publication is targeted at the UK market and as such the practices described are primarily UK focused. However, as the financial markets are global in nature, some aspects are discussed in a global context.

Overview of Investment Management

1

This chapter introduces the concept of investment management, an overview of the global market and a list of notable investment management firms.

Introduction

Investment Management entails the buying and selling of investments by investors or their agents with a view to maximising benefits to the investor. It can also be described as a process whereby investment funds (with long-term investment horizons) are managed to achieve specific objectives.

The term "investment management" is usually used interchangeably with the terms "asset management", "portfolio management" and "fund management". Most investment management firms are subsidiaries or business divisions of major financial corporations such as Deutsche Bank and usually labelled as either the asset management division, for example Deutsche Asset Management, or tagged as the investment management division as in the case of Morgan Stanley Investment Management.

Investment Management firms hire investment managers, usually referred to in the UK as fund managers, to manage investment funds. Investment managers manage funds on behalf of a firm's client base which include pension funds, investment trusts, unit trusts, OEICs (Open Ended Investment Companies) and charities. These clients are known as institutional investors and they differ from private investors that are high net worth individuals.

Private Wealth Management divisions manage the investment funds of private investors and are usually subsidiaries of major financial services firms. An example of a private wealth management division is Barclays Private Wealth Management which is a division of Barclays Bank PLC. Private Wealth Management is outside the scope of this book; it is covered in Business Knowledge for IT in Private Wealth Management.

The provision of investment management services includes elements of financial analysis, asset selection, stock selection, plan implementation and ongoing monitoring of investments.Investment management should not be confused with "investment banking" which is a totally different business that deals more with financing and trading.

A vital element in the investment management industry is regulation. In order for investors to have confidence in placing their capital with investment managers, it is necessary that they are assured that appropriate regulation is in place. Although for UK investment managers the requirements of regulatory compliance are cumbersome, the success of the UK investment management industry is due largely to the existence of a veritable and efficient regulatory framework.

Investment management is a large and important global industry in its own right responsible for handling of trillions of dollars, euros, pounds and yen. Coming under the remit of financial services many of the world's largest companies are at least in part investment managers and employ millions of staff and create billions in revenue.

Definition of Investment Management

The following are definitions of Investment Management:

■ The process of managing money, including investments, budgeting, banking, and taxes (www.Investorwords.com).
■ The management of a client's investments by a financial services company on behalf of the client giving them access to a wide range of traditional and alternative product offerings that would not be available to the average investor.

Market Value of the Global Investment Management industry

The global asset management experienced a yearly growth of 10% in 2006 with asset value hitting a record $55 trillion. This value also represents 54% on 2002 meaning that there was growth over three successive years. Growth during this period has been due to an increase in capital inflows and strong performance of equity markets.

The USA was by far the most significant region in 2005 with 48% of the world total. It was followed by Japan with 11% and the UK with 7%. The Asia-Pacific region has shown the strongest growth in recent years with 14.2 %. Countries such as China and India and regions such as the Middle East offer huge potential and many companies are showing an increased focus in these regions.

Top Twenty Global Managers

Table 1.1 Top 20 Global Managers (as at December 2004)

Organisation	Country	Total Assets (US$mn)
UBS	Switzerland	$1,975,000
Allianz Group	Germany	$1,495,323
Barclays Global Investors	UK	$1,361,949
State Street Global Advisers	USA	$1,354,330
Fidelity Investments	USA	$1,286,107
AXA Group	France	$1,185,316
Credit Suisse	Switzerland	$1,020,952
Capital Group	USA	$1,020,952
Vanguard Group	USA	$848,397
JP Morgan Chase	USA	$791,558
Deutsche Asset Management	Germany	$730,534

3

Mellon Financial	USA	$707,078
ING Investment Management	Netherlands	$671,088
Northern Trust Global	USA	$571,883
Morgan Stanley	USA	$563,208
Aviva	UK	$525,853
AIG Global Investment	USA	$524,677
IXIS Asset Management	France	$505,987
Prudential Financial	USA	$499,577
Merrill Lynch	USA	$496,171

Source: Pensions and Investment/Watson Wyatt

Overview of the UK Investment Management Industry

The UK is one of the major markets in the world for investment management along with the USA and Japan. It has a strong international disposition and attracts significant overseas funds. London is the foremost international centre for fund management.

In recent times, London has re-established itself as the world's leading financial centre for the first time since the days of the "Empire". Industry observers believe London is going from strength to strength and is outperforming the rest of the world. London has about 7% of global funds under management, is the location of 70% of the secondary bond market and almost 50% of the derivatives market.

The reason for London's inexorable rise to the summit of the global financial markets is the attraction for major global financial services companies and naturally their investment management divisions. Global investment management firms are attracted to London as result of the following factors:

- a combination of London's historic advantages and liberalised framework;
- the location halfway between Asian markets and US;
- English is the international language of global business.

As for the UK, according to International Financial Services Limited estimates, the fund management industry was responsible for a record £3.5 trillion of funds at the end of 2005 and a quarter of these funds were from overseas. Institutional funds (corporate pension funds, insurance funds etc.) account for around 66% of this figure while retail funds (unit trusts, investment trusts etc.) account for 15% or £530bn.

Advantages of UK in general as a centre for Fund Management
- Availability of highly skilled personnel and excellent professional and support services.
- Wide ranging client base: private and institutional, UK and overseas.
- Highly liquid market with the opportunity to trade in large blocks.

▓ Highly sophisticated and pioneering management styles, techniques and strategies.
▓ Track record of openness with relative accessibility to markets.
▓ A perception of UK having a fair and just business environment.
▓ Relatively solid infrastructure in telecommunications and transport links.
▓ A relatively relaxed, light-touch regulatory environment.

Largest UK Fund Management Organisations

According to the IFSL, "The UK market is relatively concentrated at the top end with the top 3 fund managers accounting for half of the pool of assets of the top 15 fund managers." There are, however, many medium and small players on the market.

Table 1.2 shows the largest UK fund management organisations.

Table 1.2 Largest UK Fund Management Organisations

Organisation	$bn
Barclays Global Investors	1,362
Aviva	526
HSBC Holdings	476
Amvescap	382
Prudential M&G	359
Legal and General Investment Managers	319
F&C Management	239
Standard Life Assurance	208
Schroders Investment Management	158
Scottish Widows Investment	158
Insight Investment Management	150
Henderson Global Investors	133
Threadneedle Asset Management	120
Hermes Pensions Management	98
Ballie Gifford	62

Source: Watson Wyatt 500, Pensions & Investments

Ownership
Mergers and acquisitions in global investment management have led to restructuring in the UK industry. A number of these activities took place between 2004 and 2006 and are as follows:

▓ F& C Management and ISIS Asset Management merged to create F&C Asset Management.

5

- Aberdeen Asset managers purchased a number of investment businesses from Deutsche Asset Management.
- ING sold Barring Asset Management to Mass Mutual.
- Framlington was acquired by AXA Investment Managers.
- Black Rock and Merrill Lynch agreed a merger.
- Legg Mason acquired Citigroup's asset management business.
- A merger between Britannic group and Resolution Life Group created Resolution Asset Management.

These deals have had limited effect on the top 10 investment managers. In this group, the firms owned by UK insurance companies continue to dominate.

Table 1.3 Top 10 Investment Managers

Companies	Parent Group	Parent Type
Barclays Global Investor Ltd	Barclays PLC	Retail Bank
Legal and General	Legal and General Group Plc	Insurance Company
Morley Fund Management	Aviva PLC	Insurance Company
M&G Securities	Prudential PLC	Insurance Company
State Street Global Advisers	State Street Corporation	Global Custodian/ Investment Services
JP Morgan Asset Management Ltd	JPM Chase & Co.	Investment bank
Standard Life Investments Ltd	Standard Life Assurance Company	Insurance Company
Scottish Widows Investment Partnership	Lloyds TSB Group PLC	Retail Bank
Insight Investment Management	HBOS PLC	Retail Bank
Fidelity International Ltd	Fidelity International	Asset Manager

Source: Investment Management Association

Staff of the Investment Management Firms

Investment management firms do not have a rigid organisational structure. The structure differs from one organisation to the next depending on factors such as size, affiliation with a parent company and the country or continent of origin, i.e. whether it is European, American or Japanese. Nevertheless, the staff listed below are typical of investment management houses:

- **Chief Executive Officer (CEO)**. Their responsibility is the general management and direction of the firm, especially the building of an effective and harmonised team to ensure profitability of the business.
- **Chief Investment Officer (CIO)**. Their responsibility includes ensuring that the firm's delivery of fund performance is competitive in the marketplace

and to promote a team-focused culture as opposed to a self-centred 'star fund manager' mindset.

- **Chief Financial Officer (CFO)**. This role is similar to that of a finance director but may involve more general administration of financial matters.
- **Chief Technology Officer**. This is the person responsible for the strategic use of IT within the investment management organisation. They decide on the strategy for sourcing of market or other data, automation of investment management processes and the use of the internet as an enabler for marketing and other processes within the organisation.
- **Marketing Director**. A recent development in the investment management sector where competition is stiffer for business from pension funds, charities etc., the marketing director is responsible for selling the company to potential clients.
- **Client liaison officer**. This person is responsible for liaising with the client on a day-to-day basis. The tasks carried out by this person include keeping in touch with the changing investment objectives of the client and reporting back to the client on the progress of the investment process, particularly as regards fund performance.
- **Senior fund manager(s)**. Senior fund managers will usually have two principal sets of responsibilities. First, they will act as the main fund managers, often making the final investment decisions (although they may simply follow the recommendations of a more junior manager) and generally playing a key role in the formulation of particular client's investment strategy. In addition to these professional duties, they will also have a managerial role, helping to run their specific desks through a variety of processes, which may include financial control, recruitment and its day-to-day management. Also, a principal function of senior managers will inevitably be the winning of new business and the attendance at presentations, meetings with potential clients and the formulation of the investment strategy of a new client.
- **Fund managers**. Fund managers may play similar roles to those of senior fund managers, but are not as involved with managerial aspects of the organisation. Their main task is management of the fund to the best of their abilities and in line with the client's strategic requirements.
- **Fund accountants**. All accounting functions related to clients' funds are the responsibility of the fund accountants. These funds are usually held in accounts controlled by the investment management firms, but are sometimes held in client-controlled accounts.
- **Custodian liaison officer**. The main responsibility of custodian officers is liaison with custodian banks to ensure safekeeping of documents relating to securities, the collection of dividends or interest payments from these securities. They are also responsible for the receipt of information on corporate actions taken by the corporation that issued the securities.
- **Dealers**. Dealers in investment management houses differ in their roles from dealers in investment banks. Investment management dealers buy or sell securities on behalf of the investment house's clients at the most favourable price available at the time of dealing while investment banking deal-

ers trade on their own account. These dealers request prices for securities from a number of brokers and select the best at the time for the lot[2] they are trading.

- **Quants**. These are highly specialised workers who usually have higher degrees in mathematical disciplines. Their role in investment management firms includes providing performance, risk and other analyses for both internal feedback and client reporting.
- **Compliance officer**. The compliance officer ensures that the organisation complies with the various legislations that affect the investment management industry. An example of legislation that should be complied with is the MiFID[3] and the Higgs Report.[4]
- **Support staff**. The support staff include administrative staff such as the company secretary, IT technical staff and other staff whose roles are in a supporting capacity to the key investment management staff.

Fundamentals of the Investment Management Function

The following are the fundamental value-adding stages of the investment management process from initial client contact through to reporting of investment activities to clients.

Stage one – initial client liaison
This is the stage when the investment manager is appointed by the client. The investment manager ascertains the client's investment objectives and then translates these into an investment strategy.

Stage two – apportioning responsibility
At this stage the investment management firm has been signed up by the client and the investment management firm decides on the roles and responsibilities and the schedules.

Stage three – research
The investment managers offer their advice to the client based on the research provided from in-house staff and third-party organisations including market data vendors and external brokers.

---

2   Multiple shares traded together, usually in units of 100.
3   MiFID – Markets in Financial Instrument Directive.
4   A report by Derek Higgs on the review of the role and effectiveness of non-executive directors.

Stage four – the decision-making process

Decisions made at this stage will provide guidelines to the investment managers as to how the funds under management will be invested and the assets and instruments to invest the funds into.

Stage five – execution of transactions

After the investment decision has been made, the investment managers are responsible for initiating the associated transactions and supervision of the ensuing transactions and settlement of the transactions. This is the case if the fund is managed on a discretionary[5] basis and is so in most cases.

Stage six – custody

Investment managers make use of custody[6] services or banks to meet a wide variety of administrative requirements and exploit money-making opportunities relating to the holding of investment instruments.

Stage seven – reporting to clients

At this stage activities include preparation and dispatch of reports to clients to provide information such as progress of the investment activity which will encompass the state of the accounts managed by the investment manager and the performance of the fund under management.

Central Task of Investment Management

The fundamental task of investment management is to construct a portfolio. To do this an investment manager ought to ensure that the institutional investor takes into account the following seven broad issues:

1. the investment objectives;
2. the investment horizon;
3. the asset classes to include in the portfolio;
4. the strategic weights to assign to these asset classes over the long term;
5. the short-term tactical weights to assign;
6. the selection strategies to use within each asset class;
7. assessment of the justification for the decisions made in steps 2–6 and how they have met the objectives.

---

5   This is a situation whereby a client gives authority to the investment manager to carry out transactions on behalf of the client without checking with the client first.
6   A financial institution that has the legal responsibility i.e. management as well as safekeeping for a customer's securities.

How Investment Management Firms Generate Revenue

Investment Management firms are obviously in business to make money so how do they generate revenue?

Investment management organisations usually charge management fees based on the percentage of the total value of the funds under management. Naturally the higher the value of the fund, the lower the percentage as there is competition amongst investment management firms for the larger funds of £25 million or above. For small funds with a value of say £300,000, the management fee that the investment management firm charges the owners of the trustees of the fund could be in the region of three-quarters of 1 per cent, while fees for larger funds, as in the case of a £25 million fund, could be about one-fifth of 1 per cent.

Other sources of revenue include mark-up commission paid to brokers whereby the client is liable for the mark-up commission.

Asset Classes

The major asset classes in investment management are as follows:

- **Cash** – when investment managers use the term cash this usually encompasses cash and near-cash i.e. assets that do not put the initial value at risk and can be turned into cash overnight. Money markets instruments such as commercial papers and Treasury bills are in this asset class.
- **Equities** – Equities are often referred to as common stock or ordinary shares and they give holders a share in the ownership of a company and also a right to participate in the company's affairs. By participation we mean that the board of directors reports to shareholders.
- **Bonds** – Bonds are debt instruments which, unlike equities, do not offer any shareholding nor participation rights. Bondholders are creditors and have to be repaid the debt owed to them in the event of liquidation. Bond issuers include companies, governments and supranational organisations like the World Bank.
- **Currency** – this is a relatively new asset class in investment management. It is traded in pairs (e.g. GBP/USD) and could potentially improve investors' return. This is discussed further in Chapter 4.
- **Property** – often referred to as 'real estate', it encompasses land and buildings. Investments in this asset class exclude homes, but include shops, offices and industrial buildings.

Major Investors

The major institutional investors in the long-term asset market can be categorised as follows:

- **Pension funds** – These are funds set up for pension plans by corporations, governments, labour unions or other organisations for their employees. An example is the Doctors' Pension Fund.
- **Insurance companies** – Insurance companies as institutional investors make large investments, often held in very large portfolios of investments in schemes such as life funds and pension funds.
- **Investment trusts** – These are companies that invest in the shares of other companies for the purpose of acting as a collective investment.
- **Unit trusts and open-ended investment companies (OEICs)** – Unit trusts are a form of collective investments constituted under a trust deed. OEICs are open-ended collective investments formed as a corporation under the Open-Ended Investment Companies Regulations. An example of a unit trust is Jupiter Unit Trust. Baillie Gifford is an example of an investment trust.
- **Charities** – Collective investments similar to unit trusts are set up by charities. Most charity funds are small and may be made up of only a bank account or probably a small holding in one of the unit trusts that are targeted at charities. Oxfam is a well-known charity that invests in schemes managed by investment managers.

Funds will be discussed in more detail in Chapter 2.

List of Some Major Investment Management Firms
The following is a list of some global investment management firms and global financial services companies that have an investment management arm:

- AXA Investment Management
- ABN AMRO Asset Management
- Allianz SE
- Barclays Global Investors
- Baring Asset Management
- Bear Stearns
- Black Rock Merrill Lynch Investment Management
- BNP Paribas Asset Management
- City Group Asset Management
- Credit Suisse Asset Management
- Deutsche Asset Management
- DnB Nor Asset Management
- Fidelity Investments
- Fortis Investments
- Gartmore Fund Managers

- Goldman Sachs Asset Management
- Henderson Global Investors
- ING Investment Management
- Insight Investment Management
- Invesco Perpetual
- Investec Asset Management
- JP Morgan Asset Management
- KBC Asset Management
- Legal & General Investment Management
- Legg Mason
- M&G
- Morgan Stanley Investment Management
- Morley Fund Management
- Old Mutual Asset Management
- Prudential Financial
- RCM - Allianz Global Investors
- Schroeders
- SG Asset Management
- State Street Global Advisors
- UBS Asset Management

Boutique Investment Management Firms

Over the last few years, institutional investors have shifted funds from larger investment management firms to the smaller and more personal boutique investment managers. 'Boutiques', as the name suggests, are upmarket, exclusive investment managers that operate in niche areas of the investment management industry.

Boutiques are mostly start-ups that are set up by people that come out of large financial institutions to offer their skills. These people leave the security and backing of the larger financial institutions to become independent and to execute their own investing philosophies and styles.

Definition of Boutique Investment Management

A boutique investment management firm can be defined as an investment management firm that is specialist, relatively small in size and manages relatively small amount of funds.

Boutiques generally focus on a limited number of asset classes or sometimes on one of them. Their independence from the influence of parent or affiliate companies within the larger financial groups removes the conflict of interest that normally arises.

For example, a big financial organisation like UBS has banking, investment banking and asset management operations that would influence the asset management arm. This is not the case with boutiques, which are focused on the business of investment management.

Characteristics of Boutique Investment Management

The following are some of the characteristics of boutique investment management companies:

- The managers of boutiques are usually the owners and they tend to carry out the day-to-day management of funds they manage.
- Clients are the only source of income for the boutiques which gives the motivation to perform, unlike bank-backed investment management firms that have the backing of their parent company.
- The lack of backing by a larger financial organisation requires the boutiques to have differentiation points to compete with the larger investment houses.
- The relative small size of boutiques allows the investment manager to be nimble, hence the ability to move in and out of markets quickly to respond to market events.
- Boutiques often outsource most of the back-room operations involving administration and investment operations to third parties, thus freeing the investment managers from administrative work for better focus on investing.
- Boutiques offer consistency in investment styles since the owner-manager isn't likely to leave the company.
- Key-man risk, often the scourge of small businesses, poses a threat to the longevity of these firms.

Advantages of Boutique Funds

- The boutiques are usually set up by the brightest and the best in the business, which has led industry watchers to infer that they offer superior service.
- Big fund managers tend to become too big to be profitable. It is argued that they have become too bureaucratic and tend to focus on matching index performance rather than exceeding it. The boutiques, in contrast, have a sharper and more coherent investment philosophy.
- There are a smaller number of analysts and portfolio managers in boutiques who tend to focus on the same kind of investment opportunities as larger fund managers and they work as a more cohesive team and exploit opportunities quickly.

Disadvantages of Boutique Funds

- Larger fund managers can offer investors diversified investment portfolios comprising multiple asset classes through a single platform.
- The investment style of the firm could be altered if one or two of the top managers leave the firm.
- Boutiques have comparatively fewer resources and less analyst armaments.
- Boutiques have smaller advertising budgets, making it difficult for investors to find them or even decide to invest in their funds.

List of some Boutique Investment Management Firms

The following are some of the top-performing investment/fund management boutiques:

13

- Midas Capital Partners
- ClariVest Asset Management
- Blue Planet
- Cartesian
- Cedar Rock Capital
- Ecofin
- Fourwinds Capital Management
- Generation Investment Management
- Lindsell Train Investment Management
- Mazuma Capital Management
- Metropole Gestion
- Oldfield Partners
- Troy
- Wolfgang Mayr

Types of Funds in Investment Management

This chapter describes the different funds in investment management, the classifications and the security identifier types and indices.

2

Introduction

Funds are the central focus of the investment management discipline and, as mentioned in Chapter 1, investment management is often referred to as fund management. The term "fund" is often used loosely in our everyday lives; we often talk about funding a car purchase or even funding a holiday. However, the discussion of funds in this chapter differs from funds in a personal context.

What is a Fund?

A fund is a mechanism for investing and managing the pooled contributions of investors for a fee. By collecting the funds of a large number of investors into specific investments (in line with the objectives of the investors), investment managers give individual investors access to a wider range of securities than the investors themselves would have been able to access. Also, individual investors should be able to save on trading costs since investment managers are able to gain economies of scale in operations.

Open-ended and closed-ended funds

Funds are classed as "open-ended" or "closed-ended" depending on whether a fund is allowed to issue and redeem shares or units on a continuous basis as in the case of open-ended funds. In this type of fund, new investors are permitted to enter and existing investors to leave the fund without restriction and these investors may also choose to increase or reduce their existing holdings. Investor holdings may fluctuate in size in an open-ended fund as opposed to a closed-ended fund that operates with a fixed amount of capital from the original launch or ensuing new issues.

In the following section, examples of open-ended funds will be discussed, such as unit trusts and OEICs. Closed-ended funds such as investment trusts and venture capital trusts will also be discussed. It should be noted that an authorised corporate director or fund manager handles dealings with new and existing investors in an open-ended fund whereas in a closed-ended fund, investors trade shares on a stock market.

Types of Funds

The various types of funds offered by investment managers are the "product range" in investment management. The performance of an investment manager is often benchmarked against their peers and it is publicised to inform the decision of investors in choosing an asset manager.

There are factors that govern the constitution of funds and their salient differences, and they include the purpose of the fund and the regulatory and tax rules that the investment manager has to abide by.

A number of common funds in the investment management market are discussed in the following section.

Life Funds

Life funds are constituted of pools of money from investors contributed to a life assurance company and invested with the aim of paying out a lump sum in the event of death or expiry over a relatively long investment horizon.

The life assurance company has legal ownership of the investments of the life fund and has the contracts known as policies with eventual beneficiaries. Benefits are paid according to the terms of each policy.

An example of a Life Fund is the Norwich Union External Life Fund.

Pension Funds

A pension fund is a pool of money established by an employer to facilitate and organise the investment of employees' retirement funds, contributed to by the employer and employees. The reason for establishing a pension fund is to generate stable growth over the long term, and provide pensions for employees when they reach the end of their working years and commence retirement. Pension funds may also provide for death-in-service benefits and widows' pensions and are often linked to a life policy provided by a life company.

One term that is associated with pensions and worth discussing is annuity, which is essentially a scheme designed to grow funds from an individual and then, upon annuitisation,[7] pay out a stream of payments to the individual at a later point in time. Annuities are mainly used as a means of securing a steady cash flow for an individual during their retirement years.

Pension schemes can also be set up as personal pensions by individuals and are regulated by regulators such as The Pensions Regulator (TPR) in the UK.

An example of a Pension Fund is Invesco Perpetual Managed Growth Pension Fund.

Unit Trusts

A unit trust is a form of collective investment scheme legally constituted under a trust deed with the aim of providing income and/or capital growth from a portfolio of investments. These investments are acquired with the pool of money contributed by the unit holders. Unit trusts are open-ended investments; therefore the underlying value of the assets is always directly represented by the total number of units issued multiplied by the unit price that is determined according to regulations minus the transaction or management fee charged.

Since unit trusts are open-ended, the fund is equitably divided into units which vary in price in direct proportion to the variation in value of the fund's net asset value[8] (NAV). Each time money is invested, new units are created to match

7 The process of converting an annuity investment into a series of periodic income payments.
8 Net Asset Value is discussed further in Chapter 5.

the prevailing unit buying price; each time units are redeemed, the assets sold match the prevailing unit selling price. In this way there is no supply or demand created for units and they remain a direct reflection of the underlying assets.

Rathbone High Income Funds is an example of a Unit Trust.

Unit trusts are very popular in the UK, Ireland, South Africa, Australia and New Zealand.

Investment Trusts

Investment trusts are not trusts as the name suggests but limited liability companies that have shareholders and, like unit trusts, funds that are invested in the shares of other companies. Instead of a trustee, investment trusts have custodians as the registered holders of the fund's investments and instead of a manager, a board of directors to manage the company.

Investment trusts enable investors to get exposure to markets that they may not be able to reach themselves (e.g. to emerging countries). Different trusts also have differing objectives (e.g. growth or income).

Unlike unit trusts, investment trusts are closed-ended funds. That is, there are a fixed number of shares in circulation, and the price of those shares is determined like other quoted shares – by supply and demand. This means that investment trust shares often trade at a discount to their NAV (i.e. the value of their underlying investments) and it also makes investment trust shares more volatile than unit trust prices.

Investment trusts are common in the UK and well-established within legal and regulatory frameworks. In other jurisdictions, similar types of closed-ended investment vehicles exist but may be known by different names.

F&C is an example of an Investment Trust.

Common Investment Funds

Common Investment Funds (CIFs) are special collective investment schemes. They operate as investment vehicles and are deemed by law to be charities themselves and are therefore eligible for registration as charities in their own right.

CIFs are similar to authorised unit trusts but, unlike unit trusts, they are not authorised by regulatory bodies such as the Financial Services Authority (FSA).

CIFs provide diversification of investment to reduce risk, which is tax-efficient, administratively simple and cost-efficient. They enjoy the same tax status as other charities.

The UK Equity Fund for Charities is an example of a Common Investment Fund.

Offshore Funds

Offshore funds are funds based outside the tax system of the country where the intended investor is residing. In the UK, the perception of offshore funds used to be that they are a high-risk, high-cost way of hiding investment assets from the UK authorities in a foreign tax haven, but not anymore. They are simply a collective scheme established outside of the UK, usually in the form of an open-ended company and issuing shares on a similar basis to the UK OEIC.

Lloyds TSB Offshore Funds Limited High Income Fund is an example of an Offshore Fund.

Index Funds

An index fund is a portfolio of investments that is weighted the same as a stock-exchange index in order to mirror its performance. This process is also referred to as "indexing" and, mathematically, it ensures that the fund achieves its aims.

Why would anyone invest in a fund that only tries to match the index rather than beat it?

Proponents of tracker funds argue that:

- Most active funds try to beat the index but the vast majority of them actually underperform it.
- A fund which can guarantee that it will do as well as the index may not be the most ambitious, but its results will be better than most other more ambitious funds.
- Because a tracker fund invests in a programmatic way, it does not need an army of analysts and researchers backing up its portfolio selection, and the costs are therefore cheaper.

HSBC FTSE All-Share Index is an example of an Index Fund.

Exchange-Traded Funds

Exchange-Traded Funds (ETFs) are funds representing a basket of stocks that reflect an index such as S&P 500 and trade on an exchange throughout the day, with intra-day pricing. Investors get the advantages of trading a diversified "basket" of stocks that reflects the performance of a market index, industry, sector, style or region – all in one security. ETFs can offer investors benefits such as tax efficiency, diversification and the ability to buy and sell throughout the trading day.

The legal structure and make-up of ETFs vary around the world; however the major common features include:

- They have an exchange listing and the ability to trade continually.
- They are index-linked rather than actively managed.
- Investors save on management fees since ETFs are passively managed.

iShares, a Barclays Global Investors' brand, is an example of an ETF and trades on more that 10 different exchanges.

Venture Capital Trusts

Venture Capital Trusts (VCTs) are a type of investment trust which invests in small unquoted companies including AIM and OFEX[9] companies, and which is designed to attract risk capital from higher-rate taxpayers by giving them tax concessions.

Like investment trusts, VCTs are quoted on the London Stock Exchange and

19

as with investment trusts, their share price may trade at a discount to net asset value.

They provide three types of tax benefit:

- 40% capital gains tax deferral provided the shares are held for a period of no less than three years.
- 20% income tax relief on the amount of the original investment.
- All dividends are tax free and all gains on disposal after three years are tax exempt. But when the shares are sold, the original capital gains tax liability will be re-triggered.

VCTs are only allowed to invest in companies under a certain size, and there is a limit on how much they can invest in any one company. The idea is that they must apply their funds to genuinely risky entrepreneurial ventures.

Northern 2 VCT PLC is an example of Venture Capital Trust.

Property Funds

Property funds are funds such as Authorised Property unit trusts that invest in the commercial real-estate sector, i.e. shopping centres, retail warehouses, urban regeneration projects, hospitals and industrial property. Another type of property fund, a Real-Estate Investment Trust (REIT), is a special tax-exempt investment vehicle.

REITs have been introduced in countries such as the UK, USA, Japan, Hong Kong and Bulgaria. The legislation concerning REITs is different from country to country. In the UK, for instance, they must be close-ended (see below) investments and publicly listed on a stock exchange recognised by the Financial Services Authority.

The legislation laying out the rules for REITs in the United Kingdom was enacted in the Finance Act 2006 and came into effect in January 2007. when many major British property companies converted from PLC status to REIT status. REITs can contain a number of properties from a wide variety of sectors, while the key advantage is that taxes are paid by the investor rather than the fund, eliminating possible double taxation. A downside to REITS, however, is that at least 90% of a REIT's net profits must be distributed to shareholders each year.

Land Securities is an example of a REIT.

Hedge Funds

Hedge Funds are investment funds that charge a performance fee and are typically open to only a limited range of investors. Hedge funds are now a $1,000bn industry and still growing at 20% per annum.

---

9   OFEX is the UK's independent public market, dedicated to smaller companies, and based on a quote-driven trading platform. Owned and operated by PLUS Markets Group plc, it is authorised and regulated by the Financial Services Authority.

Although the term "hedge" would seem to indicate that these hedge their investments against adverse market moves, the term is used to distinguish them from regulated retail investment funds such pension funds, and from insurance companies.

Hedge funds lie at the active end of the investing spectrum as they seek positive absolute returns, regardless of the performance of an index or sector benchmark. They can follow complex investment strategies, being long or short assets, and enter into futures, swaps and other derivative contracts.

GLC Partners is an example of a Hedge Fund.

Hedge funds are going to be discussed in detail in the forthcoming, "Business Knowledge for IT in Hedge Funds".

Fund of Funds

A "Fund Of Funds" (FoF) is an investment fund that uses an investment strategy of holding a portfolio of other investment funds rather than investing directly in shares, bonds or other securities. This type of investing is often referred to as multi-manager investment.

A fund of funds is characterised by diversification amongst many different funds and investment in desirable institutional funds that are off limits for retail investors.

There are different types of FoFs, each investing in a different type of collective investment scheme (typically one type per FoF). Property Fund of Funds and Fund of Hedge funds are popular types of FoFs.

Jupiter Merlin Growth Portfolio is an example of an FoF with underlying stocks that invest in equities and fixed-interest stocks across a range of geographical areas with a core holding in the UK.[10]

Fund Fact Sheet

Detailed information about a fund is presented in a fact sheet which itemises the facts or pertinent information about the fund. Below is an example of a summary section of a fund fact sheet for a fictitious fund called Bizle American Growth.

---

10 Information taken from Jupiter Asset Management:
www.jupiteronline.co.uk/PI/OurFunds/UnitTrusts/FundsofFunds/

Figure 2.1 Summary Section of Fund Fact Sheet

Fund Fact Sheet: Summary
Our initial charge: 1.00% (77.22% off standard charge)

Fund Currency	GBX	Change on Day	0.69%	Sector	North America
Bid Price	n/a	YTD return	6.03%	Fund Size (£m)	113.6
Mid Price	956.6	Yield	0.00%	Fund Type	OEIC
Offer price	n/a	Type	Growth	Launch Date	30-06-1999

Fund Objective
This fund aims for capital growth from a portfolio of North American securities. The historical track record reflects the Bizle North American Unit Trust. Long-term performance is based on the Bizle North American Unit Trust launched on 01-03-1983.

Fund Rating[11]

FT Fund Rating		Financial Express Crown Rating
Risk Level	n/a	n/a
Performance	n/a	

Performance Against Sector

Total returns	Fund+/-	Sector+/-
1 year	+11.92%	+9.39%
2 year	+23.04%	+25.62%
3 year	+0.89%	+5.23%

12 Month Performance

High	957.00
Low	816.50

Fund Performance

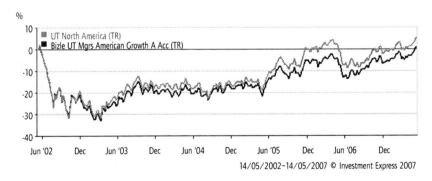

14/05/2002–14/05/2007 © Investment Express 2007

11 Fund ratings could also be from OSBR, S&P Research or Lipper.
12 Companies with market capitalisation of $5 billion or more.

Manager Information

Name	Start Date	Biography
North American Equities Team	30-06-1999	Ben Bigfoot is the head of North American equities responsible for the management of Bizle's North American equity investments. Ben joined the company in 2001 from Tank Pension Fund where he worked in Asian equities, focusing on large-cap[12] stocks.

Current Market Information

Bid	n/a
Mid	956.6
Offer	n/a
Change	6.6(0.69%)
Price Date	21-05-2007

Purchase Information

		Charges	
Min. Single Investment	20	Standard (Fund Manager) Initial Charge	4.25%
Min. Regular Savings	20		
Ex-Dividend Date(s)	1 May 1 Oct	Interactive Investor Initial Charge	1.00% (77.22% off standard charge)
ISA	Yes	Annual Management Charge	1.5%
PEP	Yes		

Fund Codes

ISIN Code	GB00C0YXP123[13]
MEX Code[14]	AGAMLA

The fact sheet usually contains other information such as the Fund Performance by Calendar Year and Fund price movement. The holding information, such as company stock that constitutes the fund, and sector weighting is also included.

Associated Costs

There are obviously costs involved in managing the fund described above, either to the investors or to the manager. Investor costs, known as charges, can be found on a Fund Fact Sheet as shown above.

13 Fictitious ISIN code.
14 The Financial Times' coding system for investment funds.

Investor Costs

Costs to investors include the following:

- Initial charge – also known as "front-end" or "sales" charge – is an amount or percentage added to the cost of buying units.
- Exit charge – also known as "back-end" or "redemption" charge – is an amount or percentage subtracted from the earnings from a sale of units.
- Annual charge – is an amount or percentage of Net Asset Value subtracted from the fund's income or capital depending on the circumstances.

IMA Sector Definitions and Classification

The Investment Management Association (IMA) has devised a fund classification system to help investors select funds and compare them with like funds. This system defines some 30 sector categories, divided into funds that aim to provide an "income", those designed to provide "growth" and the specialist fund. Each sector is made up of funds investing in similar assets, or the same stock-market sectors, or in the same geographical region.

The fund classification aids investors in realising their investment objectives and ensuring that, when comparing one fund with another, investors compare funds with similar objectives or with similar underlying assets.

UK Sector Classification

Figure 2.2 Sector Classification

All Funds

Income Funds		Growth Funds		Specialist Fund
Immediate Income	Growing Income	Capital Protection	Capital Growth/ Total Return	Specialist
UK Gilts	UK Equity Income	Money Market	UK All Companies	Specialist
UK Index Linked Gilts		Protected/ Guaranteed Funds	UK Smaller Companies	Technology and Telecommunications
UK Corporate Bond			Japan	Personal Pensions
UK Other Bond			Japanese Smaller Companies	

Global Bonds UK Equity & Bond Income	Asia Pacific Including Japan
	Asia Pacific Excluding Japan
	North America
	North American Smaller
	Europe Including UK
	Europe Excluding UK
	European Smaller Companies
	Cautious Managed
	Balanced Managed
	Active Managed
	Global Growth
	Global Emerging Markets
	UK Zeros

Source: Investment Management Association

Further description of these sector definitions is available in the Appendix.

Creation of Funds

Investment managers take a number of factors into consideration when establishing new funds. While these factors may be obvious, it is worth noting the motivations for creating funds.

Some of the factors include:

- sufficient investor interest in the type of fund to be established;
- whether to target the fund at the retail market or the wholesale market;
- the main investment objective of the fund, i.e. whether it is to generate high levels of income or go for capital appreciation;
- the tax ramifications for the parties involved, i.e. manager and investors.

25

Investment managers gain the required authorisation to market a new fund to the public and submit the documents that establish the fund's structure as a company or trust to the relevant authorities in the countries that intend to market the fund. The authority in the UK is the Financial Services Authority (FSA) and the process of authorisation for funds is representative of most authorities.

Other documents submitted to the authorities include the fund prospectus or any similar document that details the charging structure, objectives, policies and other operating arrangements. Also submitted are an official request for authorisation, a fee and a marketing plan.

After the fund has been authorised, it is launched, i.e. a number of units or shares are initially offered to investors. Prior to the launch, the necessary administrative and management procedures and systems are in place, operational and able to cope with the anticipated volumes.

Indices

What are Indices?
Definition
Indices are statistical indicators providing a representation of the value of the securities which constitute them. Indices often serve as barometers for a given market or industry and benchmarks against which financial or economic performance is measured (Investorwords.com).

FTSE
The FTSE 100 Index (pronounced *footsie*) is a share index of the 100 largest companies listed on the London Stock Exchange which meet a number of requirements set out by the FTSE Group. The requirements include having a full listing on the London Stock Exchange with Sterling or Euro dominated price on SETS, and meeting certain tests on nationality, free float and liquidity.

The index is seen as a barometer of success of the British economy and is the leading share index in Europe. It is maintained by the FTSE Group, now an independent company which originated as a joint venture between the *Financial Times* and the London Stock Exchange (hence the abbreviation Financial Times Stock Exchange). According to the FTSE Group's website, the FTSE 100 companies represent about 80% of the UK share market.

Major World Stock Market Indices
- DAX 30 – Germany
- CAC 40 – France
- Euro Stoxx – European
- SMI – Switzerland
- MIB 30 – Italy
- IBEX35 – Spain
- Dow Jones – USA

- S&P 500 – USA
- Nasdaq 100 – USA
- Nikkei 225 – Japan
- Hang Seng - Hong Kong

MSCI Europe Index

The MSCI Europe Index is a free float-adjusted market capitalisation index that is designed to measure developed market equity performance in Europe. As of June 2006, the MSCI Europe Index consisted of the following 16 developed market country indices: Austria, Belgium, Denmark, Finland, France, Germany, Greece, Ireland, Italy, the Netherlands, Norway, Portugal, Spain, Sweden, Switzerland and the United Kingdom.

Goldman Sachs Commodity Index

The Goldman Sachs Commodity Index (GSCI) is a world-production weighted index comprising 24 commodity futures contracts. The index is a composite index of commodity sector returns and represents an unleveraged investment through broadly diversified long positions in commodity futures. The GSCI primarily serves as a benchmark for investment in the commodity markets and as a measure of commodity performance over time. It is a tradable index that is readily available to market participants of the Chicago Mercantile Exchange. The GSCI was developed and is calculated by Goldman Sachs. Futures of the GSCI use a multiple of 250.

iTraxx

iTraxx is a family of Credit Default Swap indices products. The main index is the DJ iTraxx Investment Grade index covering 125 European credits. The index is rolled every six months based on a set of rules.

The prices for these indices are set by market demand as they are tradable instruments in their own right with predetermined fixed rates. Markit Group collects the official pricing on behalf of the International Index Company (IIC) on a daily basis by polling trading desks at banks that are licensed market makers.[15]

Whilst at present trading in iTraxx indices is limited to the over-the-counter (OTC) market, Eurex, the futures exchange, is to launch exchange-traded futures contracts based upon the iTraxx Europe, HiVol and Crossover 5 Year indices.

iTraxx Europe Series 7 is used by investment managers across Europe.

Arithmetic of Indices

Indices measure changes over time and this is achieved by calculating the aggregate of the values of its individual constituents at the start of a base date and expressing the result as a base number, usually 100 or 1000.

---

15   A brokerage or bank that maintains a firm bid and ask price in a given security and in apposition to buy or sell at publicly quoted prices.

Indices are usually constructed in different ways but the most common ways are arithmetic, geometric and weighted arithmetic. For the sake of simplicity, the arithmetic method will be examined in this section.

The formula for a simple arithmetic index is as follows:

$$\frac{\text{Sum of prices at the current date}}{\text{Sum of prices at the base date}} * \text{Base number}$$

Example

To construct a fictitious index, Biz Stock Average, the simple aggregate of prices of each share that constitute the index at 2 January (base date) is £1440 and at 20 December (current date) the aggregate is £1550. Using 2 February as the base date and selecting 1000 as the base number, the 20 December index will be:

$$\frac{1550}{1440} * 1000 = 1,076.39$$

Dow Jones Industrial Index and the Nikkei Stock Average are examples of simple arithmetic indices.[16]

Security Identifier Types

Security Identifiers should be mentioned in this section as they are used to iden-tify either bonds or shares that are traded by the banks.

Definition

Security identifier types are the various methods by which a security product or issue is identified. They are each managed and distributed by different organi-sations.

Three different types that are commonly adopted in the UK will be discussed.

ISIN

An International Securities Identifying Number (ISIN) – pronounced *icing* – uniquely identifies a security. Its structure is defined in ISO 6166. Securities for which ISINs are issued include bonds, commercial paper, equities and warrants. The ISIN code is a 12-character alpha-numerical code that does not contain information characterising financial instruments but serves for uniform identifi-cation of a security at trading and settlement.

ISINs are created only for securities and not derivatives such as options or futures. Additionally, securities offered on more than one stock exchange will

16   http://www.brajeshwar.com/business/stock/stock-market-index.html

use the same ISIN, which can make it problematic when trading in Europe where this is common.

CUSIP

The acronym CUSIP typically refers to both the Committee on Uniform Security Identification Procedures and the 9-digit alphanumeric security identifiers that they distribute for all North American securities for the purposes of facilitating clearing and settlement of trades. The CUSIP distribution system is owned by the American Bankers Association and is operated by Standard & Poor's. The CUSIP Services Bureau acts as the National Numbering Association (NNA) for North America, and the CUSIP serves as the National Securities Identification Number for products issued from both the United States and Canada.

RIC

A Reuters Instrument Code, or RIC, is a ticker-like code used by Reuters to identify financial instrument types and indices. RIC codes use "artificial" tickers for common indexes and money market instruments. For instance, the US 10-year money market bond is assigned the ticker US10YT, the "T" at the end referring to "Treasury". Commodities are similarly assigned tickers, for instance crude oil is CL. Indexes have a leading period, for instance .DJI is the Dow Jones Industrial Average.

The Business Environment in Investment Management

This chapter describes the business environment in which investment management firms operate and encompasses the major players, the allied industries and regulators.

Introduction

The business environment in which investment management firms operate is shaped by the key economic factors that include the following:

- interest rates;
- money supply;
- exchange rate;
- inflation;
- government fiscal policy;
- use of technology.

Interest Rates

Movements in interest rates can make a currency more attractive or unattractive to international investors. They could also impact on the cost of borrowing and lending.

Impact: Interest rate movements affect the prices of the stocks and bonds and hence stimulate or dampen securities trading. This will also affect the price of commercial property and affect the performance of property funds.

Inflation and Money Supply

Too much spending by a country's government can lead to excess growth in the money supply, and inflation, which erodes the value of the currency.

Impact: This will have an adverse effect on revaluation of foreign assets in the investment manager's portfolio.

Government Fiscal Policy

A government's fiscal stance will have a significant effect on the international standing of the local currency. If the government runs a budget deficit by spending more than it collects in tax revenues, the difference is made good by borrowing on the domestic or capital markets. Too much borrowing can lead to rising interest rates, which slow down economic growth and tend to adversely affect the market value of investment assets such as fixed income bonds and equities and make the local currency less attractive as an investment vehicle.

Impact: Portfolios that contain fixed income securities will be impacted by the increased cost of borrowing. Slowdown in economic growth will impact of the retail investment management sector as private investors have less disposable income.

Exchange Rates

The movements in the exchange rate of currency pairs are dependent mainly on interest rates and trade balance. Demand and supply of currencies dictate the

31

exchange rate of one currency against the other. A currency will tend to become more valuable whenever demand for it is greater than the available supply. It will become less valuable whenever demand is less than the available supply (this does not mean people no longer want money, it just means they prefer holding their wealth in some other form, possibly another currency).

Impact: The increasing importance of currency as an asset class will be impacted as currency portfolio managers have to manage exchange rate exposures. Property investment managers and investors are impacted by currency fluctuations as they affect the value of their property holdings in the international real-estate market.

Stock Market
The stock market is the market for the trading of company stock, and a derivative of the same. The global stock market is governed by the conventional market mechanism, i.e. demand and supply.

Impact: Investment managers generate revenue from proprietary trading on the stock markets.

Use of Technology
Most of the recent advancements with trading have been due to new technology such as algorithmic trading. Also the growth of the internet has made tools and data such as analyst recommendations, estimates and first call revisions, news feeds, charts, trading oscillators, market forecasts and insider trading available instantly online.

The use of the internet for marketing to and dealing by investors makes physical location less of a consideration for managers, but raises obvious issues for regulation of firms and funds operating on the web.

Impact: With increasing use of technology, investment managers make better investment and trading decisions and investors become more knowledgeable about the market.

Players in Investment Management

The business environment is made up of the following players:

- central banks;
- the competitors (other investment managers and hedge funds);
- the exchanges – for example the London Stock Exchange;
- allied organisations, i.e. the regulators, credit agencies, new agencies, clearing houses.

Exchanges and Government Central Banks

London Stock Exchange

The London Stock Exchange is a stock exchange located in London. Founded in 1801, it is one of the largest stock exchanges in the world, with many overseas listings as well as UK companies.

The LSE is broken down into the Main Market and Alternative Investments Market (AIM), as well as EDX London (which handles derivatives). The independent FTSE Group maintains a series of indices for measuring the LSE, including the FTSE 100 Index, FTSE 250 Index and FTSE 350 Index.

European Central Bank

The European Central Bank (ECB) is in Frankfurt am Main. Germany is the central bank of the eurozone, in charge of monetary policy for the 12 countries that use the euro currency. The ECB's main task is to maintain the euro's purchasing power and thus price stability in the euro area. The ECB was established on 1 June 1998.

The central bank is the sole issuer of banknotes and bank reserves. That means it is the monopoly supplier of the monetary base. By virtue of this monopoly, it can set the conditions at which banks borrow from the central bank.

The Competitors

The UK investment management sector consists mainly of firms whose headquarters are either in the USA, Japan, the Netherlands, France or Germany.

Overview of the Major Players in Investment Management

UBS AG

UBS is a diversified global financial services company that specialises in investment banking, asset management, wealth management and retail and commercial banking in Switzerland. It is headquartered in Basel and Zurich and is also has offices in all major financial centres worldwide.

UBS Global Asset Management provides investment products and services to private clients, financial intermediaries and institutional investors around the world. It is one of the largest global institutional asset managers.

Some data on UBS includes:

- net profit CHF12,257 million;
- invested assets CHF2,989 billion;
- number of employees 78,140.

Allianz SE

Allianz SE is a financial services company that provides asset management, banking and insurance services and is the parent company of Allianz Group. The range of services encompasses the property and casualty insurance, banking and asset management segments.The headquarters of the company is in Munich, Germany.

The instituitional asset management division manages assets belonging to institutions such as corporations, states and local governments and these represent two thirds of the assets under their management.

Some data on Allianz includes:

- operating profit €10,386 million;
- third-party assets under management €736,855 million;
- number of employees 166,505.

State Street Corporation

State Street is a provider of financial services to institutional investors. The range of services includes fund accounting, custody, research, investment management, trading services, transfer agency services and operations outsourcing for investment managers. State Street is headquartered in Boston, Massachusetts and maintains operations in 26 countries covering all major investment centres.

Some data on State Street:

- revenue $1.7 billion (Q1 2007);
- total assets under management $1.7 trillion;
- number of employees 21,700 (as at December 2006).

Barclays PLC

Barclays is a UK-based financial services group that is engaged primarily in banking, investment banking and investment management. Barclays' operations include Barclays Global Investors (investment management), Barclays Capital (investment banking) and Barclays Wealth (private wealth management).

Barclays Global Investors provides investment management services to 2,900 institutional investors in 52 countries and is well-known in investment circles as being at the forefront of developing innovative investment ideas.

Some data on Barclays PLC includes:

- profit before tax £7,136million;
- total assets under management £907 billion;
- number of employees 123,000.

Investment Management Association

The Investment Management Association (IMA) is the trade body for the £2,800 billion UK investment management industry, which has the largest assets under management in Europe. Its members provide investment management services to institutions and private investors through individual fund management agreements and pooled products such as authorised investment funds.

The IMA's main responsibility is to promote a legal, regulatory and tax environment that is conducive to the requirements of the asset managers and their clients and it also helps to maintain the reputation of the investment management industry.

Government regulators, other policy makers, and the press in the UK and across the European continent work with the IMA, which acts as the representative voice of the industry. The association provides a centre of excellence for the development of knowledge and understanding of investment management.

The IMA publishes market statistics and rankings of the UK fund management industry on a monthly and quarterly basis. The table below shows the February 2007 monthly ranking of UK Fund Management industry.

Table 3.1 Ranking of UK Fund Management industry

Ranking	Company	Total Funds Under Management Value
1	Fidelity Investments Limited	£30,605,509,000
2	Invesco Perpetual	£25,346,417,344
3	SLTM	£24,141,343,060
4	Legal & General Investment Management	£21,656,525,027
5	Resolution Asset Management Limited	£20,023,916,749
6	Threadneedle Investment Services Ltd	£17,488,323,911
7	Halifax Investment Fund Managers Ltd	£17,188,670,744
8	Schroder Investment Management Ltd	£17,124,577,443
9	Scottish Widows Unit Trusts Managers	£15,742,774,697
10	M & G Securities Limited	£14,310,555,509

Source: Investment Management Association

Allied Organisations

Allied organisations to the investment banking industry include the regulators, the news agencies, the clearing houses and credit rating agencies. The following are some of the allied organisations that service the UK investment management industry.

The Regulators

Bank of England
The Bank of England is the central bank of the United Kingdom and has two core purposes – monetary stability and financial stability. The bank has the legislative responsibility, through the Monetary Policy Committee, to set the UK's

official interest rate and is also responsible for the issuing of banknotes. Apart from the monetary and financial stability roles, the bank works closely with financial markets and institutions to collate and publish monetary and banking statistics.

The Bank of England was established in 1694 to be the UK government's bank and since the late 18th century has been the bank to the banking system. It is based in Threadneedle Street in the heart of London's "square mile" and is sometimes referred to as the "Old Lady" of Threadneedle Street.

Financial Services Authority

The Financial Services Authority (FSA) is an independent non-departmental public and quasi-judicial body that regulates the financial services industry in the United Kingdom. Its main office is based in Canary Wharf, London, with another office in Edinburgh. When acting as the competent authority for the listing of shares on a stock exchange, it is referred to as the UK Listing Authority (UKLA) and maintains the Official List.

The FSA's main role in the investment banking community is to regulate the banks as well as reduce financial crime. Investment banks have to comply with sets of regulations that govern the financial industry and have a requirement to report their activities to the FSA.

Bank for International Settlements

The Bank for International Settlements (or BIS) is an international organisation of central banks which exists to *"foster cooperation among central banks and other agencies in pursuit of monetary and financial stability"*. The BIS also provides banking services, but only to central banks or to international organisations like itself.

The BIS, based in Basle, Switzerland, was established in 1930 and is the world's oldest international financial organisation.

Accounting and Auditing Organisation for Islamic Financial Institutions

The Accounting and Auditing Organisation for Islamic Financial Institutions (AAOIFI) is an Islamic, international, autonomous, non-profit-making corporate body that prepares accounting, auditing, governance, ethics and Shari'a standards for Islamic financial institutions.

AAOIFI was established in accordance with the Agreement of Association which was signed by Islamic financial institutions on 1 Safar 1410H, corresponding to 26 February 1990, in Algiers. AAOIFI was registered on 11 Ramadan 1411 corresponding to 27 March 1991 in the State of Bahrain.

The objective of the AAOIFI – within the Islamic Shari'a rules and principles – includes developing accounting, auditing, governance and ethical thought relating to the activities of Islamic financial institutions, taking into consideration the international standards and practices, to ensure compliance with Islamic Shari'a rules.

The Committee of European Securities Regulators (CESR)

CESR is an independent Committee of European Securities Regulators. It was established under the terms of the European Commission's decision of 6 June 2001.The role of the CESR includes improvement of co-ordination among securities regulators and acting as an advisory group to assist the EU commission.

The FSA in the UK, the Financial Regulator, and the European Commission in Belgium are some of the key members of the CESR.

Electronic Communication Networks (ECN)

Electronic communication networks (ECNs) are fully automated systems that match orders and set prices for trades. In a certain sense, an ECN functions very much like an electronic stock exchange although, from a strictly regulatory perspective, ECNs are not exchanges. The primary products that are traded on ECNs are stocks and currencies.

In order to trade with an ECN, one must be a subscriber. ECN subscribers can enter limit orders into the ECN, usually via a custom computer terminal or a direct dial-up. The ECN will post those orders on the system for other subscribers to view. The ECN will then match contra-side orders (i.e. a sell-order is "contra-side" to a buy-order with the same price and share count) for execution. Generally, the buyer and seller are anonymous, with the trade execution reports listing the ECN as the party.

Some ECNs may offer additional features to subscribers such as negotiation or reserve size, and may have access to the entire ECN book (as opposed to the "top of the book") that contains important real-time market data regarding depth of trading interest.

The rise of ECNs is having a dramatic effect on investment management business processes in that it allows the investment managers to bypass brokers and permits buyers and sellers to interact directly. As a trading channel, it is integrated with their in-house order management systems using standard industry formats to facilitate seamless order flow directly to and from portfolio managers.

Investment managers in recent times have been turning to trading via ECNs for best execution, efficiency and compliance with regulation such as MiFID. Instinet, TradeBook and NexTrade are some of the major ECNs for investment managers.

Liquidity Pools

In recent times, the search for liquidity has been at the centre of the buy-side trading process and as a result, institutional traders are seeking out large liquidity pools to execute large trades while maintaining anonymity. As a consequence, institutional traders are applying ever more sophisticated tools such as algorithms and smart routing technologies to address, among other issues, the dispersion of liquidity across regional exchanges and ECNs as well as an increase in the level of non-displayed liquidity.

Liquidity pools are an initiative taken up by the investment industry with a view to matching orders on a continuous and anonymous basis. According to Financial News, the number of dark liquidity pools has more than doubled to more than 40 since the start of 2007. *"Many are crossing networks of one form or another that match buyers and sellers anonymously, minimising information leakage and market impact, often with lower trading costs."*

A host of the major players in the global financial services industry have established liquidity pools. Among them are the following:

- VortEx – owned by Bank of New York's BNY ConvergEx Group;
- Sigma X – Goldman Sachs' liquidity pool;
- BlockAlert – a Merrill Lynch and Investment Technology Group initiative.

Consortia of financial services firms are also launching liquidity pools. Notable ones include Block Interest Discovery Service, Bids, which is accessible to the buy-side community wanting to trade large blocks, and LeveL, which allows firms to choose whether to cross their own order flow or look to match against those from other firms using the system.[17]

The Credit Rating Agencies

A credit rating agency (CRA) is a company that assigns credit ratings for issuers of certain types of debt obligations. In most cases, these issuers are companies, cities, non-profit organisations, or national governments issuing debt-like securities that can be traded on a secondary market. A credit rating measures credit worthiness (the ability to pay back a loan) and affects the interest rate applied to loans. Interest rates are not the same for everyone but instead are based on risk-based pricing, a form of price discrimination based on the different expected costs of different borrowers, as set out in their credit rating. There exist more than 100 rating agencies worldwide.

Uses of Credit Rating Agencies
Credit ratings are used by investors, issuers, investment banks, broker-dealers and governments. For investors, credit rating agencies increase the range of investment alternatives and provide independent, easy-to-use measurements of relative credit risk; this generally increases the efficiency of the market, lowering costs for both borrowers and lenders. This in turn increases the total supply of risk capital in the economy, leading to stronger growth.

Moody's
Moody's Corporation is the holding company for Moody's Investors Service, which performs financial research and analysis on commercial and government

17 Source: "Dark liquidity pools make a splash with US traders" *Financial News* 25 April 2007.

entities. The company also ranks the credit-worthiness of borrowers using a standardised ratings scale. The company has a 40% share in the world credit rating market.

Moody's Ratings

Long-term Obligation Ratings

Moody's long-term obligation ratings are opinions of the relative credit risk of fixed-income obligations with an original maturity of one year or more. They address the possibility that a financial obligation will not be honoured as promised. Such ratings reflect both the likelihood of default and any financial loss suffered in the event of default.

Investment grade

Table 3.2 Investment grade credit ratings

Rating(s)	Description
Aaa	Obligations rated Aaa are judged to be of the highest quality, with minimal credit risk.
Aa1, Aa2, Aa3	Obligations rated Aa are judged to be of high quality and are subject to very low credit risk.
A1, A2, A3	Obligations rated A are considered upper-medium grade and are subject to low credit risk.
Baa1, Baa2, Baa3	Obligations rated Baa are subject to moderate credit risk. They are considered medium-grade and as such may possess certain speculative characteristics.

Speculative grade

Table 3.3 Speculative grade credit ratings

Rating(s)	Description
Ba1, Ba2, Ba3	Obligations rated Ba are judged to have speculative elements and are subject to substantial credit risk.
B1, B2, B3	Obligations rated B are considered speculative and are subject to high credit risk.
Caa1, Caa2, Caa3	Obligations rated Caa are judged to be of poor standing and are subject to very high credit risk.
Ca	Obligations rated Ca are highly speculative and are likely in, or very near, default, with some prospect of recovery of principal and interest.
C	Obligations rated C are the lowest rated class of bonds and are typically in default, with little prospect for recovery of principal or interest.

Special

D   (in default), WR (withdrawn rating), NR (not rated), P (Provisional).

Short-term Ratings

Moody's short-term ratings are opinions of the ability of issuers to honour short-term financial obligations. Ratings may be assigned to issuers, short-term programmes or to individual short-term debt instruments. Such obligations generally have an original maturity not exceeding 13 months, unless explicitly noted.

Moody's employs the following designations to indicate the relative repayment ability of rated issuers:

Table 3.4 Speculative grade credit ratings

Rating(s)	Description
P-1	Issuers (or supporting institutions) rated Prime-1 have a superior ability to repay short-term debt obligations.
P-2	Issuers (or supporting institutions) rated Prime-2 have a strong ability to repay short-term debt obligations.
P-3	Issuers (or supporting institutions) rated Prime-3 have an acceptable ability to repay short-term obligations.
NP	Issuers (or supporting institutions) rated Not Prime do not fall within any of the Prime rating categories.

Standard and Poor's

Standard & Poor's (S&P) is a subsidiary of McGraw-Hill that publishes financial research and analysis on stocks and bonds. It is one of the top three players in this business, along with Moody's and Fitch Ratings.

It is well-known for its US-based S&P 500 and the Australian S&P 200 stock market index.

Credit ratings

As a credit rating agency, Standard & Poor's issues credit ratings for the debt of companies. As such, it is designated a Nationally Recognised Statistical Rating Organisation by the US Securities and Exchange Commission.

It issues both short-term and long-term credit ratings.

Long-term Credit Ratings

Investment Grade

Table 3.5 Investment grade credit ratings

Rating(s)	Description
AAA	The best-quality companies, reliable and stable
AA	Quality companies, a bit higher risk than AAA
A	Economic situation can affect finance
BBB	Medium-class companies, which are satisfactory at the moment

Non-Investment Grade (also known as junk bonds)

Table 3.6 Non-Investment Grade credit ratings

Rating(s)	Description
BB	More prone to changes in the economy
B	Financial situation varies noticeably
CCC	Currently vulnerable and dependent on favourable economic conditions to meet its commitments
CC	Highly vulnerable, very speculative bonds
C	Highly vulnerable, perhaps in bankruptcy or in arrears but still continuing to pay out on obligations
CI	Past due on interest
R	Under regulatory supervision owing to its financial situation
SD	Has selectively defaulted on some obligations
D	Has defaulted on obligations and S&P believes that it will generally default on most or all obligations
NR	Not rated

News Agencies and Data Providers

What are News Agencies?

A news agency is an organisation of journalists established to supply news reports to organisations in the news trade: newspapers, magazines, and radio and television broadcasters. They are also known as wire services or news services.

News agencies can be corporations that sell news, co-operatives composed of newspapers that share their articles with each other, or commercial newswire services which charge organisations to distribute their news. Governments may

41

also control "news agencies", particularly in authoritarian states like China and the Soviet Union. A recent rise in internet-based alternative news agencies, as a component of the larger alternative media, have emphasised a "non-corporate view" as being largely independent of the pressures of business media.

News agencies generally prepare hard news stories and feature articles that can be used by other news organisations with little or no modification, and then sell them to other news organisations. They provide these articles in bulk electronically through wire services (originally they used telegraphy; today they frequently use the internet). Corporations, individuals, analysts and intelligence agencies may also subscribe. The business proposition of news agencies might thus be responsible for the current trends in separation of fact-based reporting from Op-eds.[18]

The following are notable news agencies and market data providers that service the investment management industry.

Reuters

Reuters Group plc was founded in 1851 and is best known as a news service that provides reports from around the world to newspapers and broadcasters. However, news reporting accounts for less than 10% of the company's income. Its main focus is on supplying the financial markets with information and trading products. These include market data, such as share prices and currency rates, research and analytics, as well as trading systems that allow dealers to buy and sell such things as currencies and shares on a computer screen instead of by telephone or on a trading floor like that of the New York Stock Exchange.

Reuters has 2,400 journalists based in 131 countries and is the largest information provider in the world, serving 330,000 professionals.

Lipper, a Reuters company, supplies mutual fund information, analytical tools, and commentary to the investment management community. Lipper's benchmarking provides a guideline to asset managers, fund companies, financial intermediaries, traditional media, websites, and individual investors.

Bloomberg

Bloomberg L.P. is a financial news service founded by Michael Bloomberg in 1981. It provides real-time and archived financial and market data, pricing, trading, news and communications tools in a single, integrated package to corporations, news organisations, financial and legal professionals, and individuals around the world using the Bloomberg terminal and Bloomberg media services.

Bloomberg has grown to include a global news service, including television, radio, the internet and publications. The financial newswire service, Bloomberg News, comprises 1,600 reporters in 94 bureaus worldwide, writing more than 4,000 news stories daily.

18 Op-eds are pieces of writing expressing an opinion.

Financial Express

Financial Express is a data company which specialises in the collection, validation, dissemination and analysis of fund information within data feeds, documentation, web pages and internet-based fund selection tools. Financial Express supplies more than half of all UK fund management companies.

Financial Express fund data collection service collects fund prices, dividends, histories, and fact-sheet data for UK and offshore funds. It provides an additional layer of research and analysis technology to help its customers and to educate and inform fund management professionals, financial advisers and investors.

Financial Express data collection includes:

- UK, European and global investment funds, pension funds, life insurance, offshore funds, offshore life insurance, investment trusts and hedge funds;
- prices, dividends, corporate actions (capital events) and histories;
- fact-sheet information – holdings, sector/region weightings and manager biographies;
- asset allocations.

Bloomberg, Reuters and Thomson and other leading market data vendors are the recipients of data distribution from Financial Express.

Markit

Markit Group Limited is a provider of independent, multi-asset class, high-value services for the global financial market. The company provides independent pricing, reference data, portfolio valuations, trade processing and desktop solutions that are used by investment managers around the world to enhance trading operations, monetise data, reduce risk and manage compliance initiatives.

Markit has data contributed by over 60 dealing firms, and its services are used by 400 institutions globally. Areas of product expertise include OTC derivatives (credit, equity, FX, rates, inflation, energy, power, metals and structured products), corporate bonds, syndicated loans, dividend forecasting, and index and ETF management.

The Financial Times

The Financial Times (FT) is an international business newspaper printed on distinctive salmon-pink broadsheet paper. The periodical is printed in 22 cities: London, Leeds, Dublin, Paris, Frankfurt, Stockholm, Milan, Madrid, New York, Chicago, LA, San Francisco, Dallas, Atlanta, Miami, Washington DC, Tokyo, Hong Kong, Singapore, Seoul, Dubai and Johannesburg.

FTfm

FTfm is a managed fund service that comprises data collected by FT Interactive Data and MoneyMate for the investment management sector. The lists of funds grouped together by fund management companies are published weekly in the *Financial Times* and these include:

- Authorised Investment Funds and OEICs;
- FSA recognised funds;
- Regulated funds.

The types of data published for each fund include:

- **Initial Charge** – Charges made by manager/operator to the buyer. Used to settle marketing and administrative costs, including commission paid to intermediaries.
- **Buying (Offer) Price** – This is the price at which units in a unit trust are bought by investors. It includes the manager's initial charge.
- **Selling (Bid) Price** – This is the price at which units in a unit trust are sold by investors.
- **Fund rating** – funds are assigned ratings (from 1 to 5) to three aspects of funds which are shown under the headings:
  - **Risk (R)**, measured by volatility.[19] 1 is very low risk, 2 low risk, 3 medium risk, 4 high risk and 5 very high risk.
  - **Charges (C)**. 1 indicates very low charges, 2 low charges, 3 medium charges, 4 high charges and 5 very high charges.
  - **Past Performance (P)** measured relative to a fund's risk profile. 1 indicates very low performance, 2 low performance, 3 medium performance, 4 high performance and 5 very high performance.

An illustration is shown below.

A fictitious company, Biz Investment Management, could have its equity funds displayed in the Managed Fund Service as follows:

	Init Chg	Selling Price	Buying Price	+or	Ratings R C P
Biz Investment Management					
2 Ess Street, London S1 4XX					
Equities					
Eastern European Equity	51/4		€84.02	-0.15	3 4 5
India Equity A USD	51/4		$55.66	-1.88	1 2 3

Morgan Stanley Capital International (MCSI)

Morgan Stanley International Inc. is a global provider of equity (US and International) fixed income and hedge fund indices. MSCI provides global equity indices which, over the last 30+ years, have become the most widely used international equity benchmarks by institutional investors. MSCI constructs global equity benchmark indices that contribute to the investment process by serving as relevant and accurate performance benchmarks and effective research tools, and as the basis for various investment vehicles.

19   A statistical measure of the distribution of returns for a given security or market index.

Close to 2,000 organisations worldwide currently use the MSCI international equity benchmarks. MSCI estimates that over USD3 trillion are currently benchmarked to these indices on a worldwide basis.

MCSI also provides a wide range of fixed income indices for the investment community, including indices for Sovereign, Investment Grade and High Yield debt markets, as well as the Interest Rate Swaps market.

Investment Property Databank

IPD is a global information business, dedicated to the supply of independent market indices, portfolio benchmarks and detailed research to the property industry. Through its portfolio analysis service it helps investment management clients measure the performance of their real estate portfolios and to benchmark themselves against their peers.

The service also offers the following benefits:

- Accentuates the strengths and weaknesses of fund's performance.
- Provides an independent audit of performance in full accordance with Global Investment Performance (GIPS)*.
- Appraises the effectiveness of property management.
- Analyses the efficiencies of property management.
- Identifies the impact of market sector allocation and stock selection.
- Illustrates investment returns in detail for all types of property investment, both directly and indirectly owned.

IPD constructs indices, aptly named "IPD Indices", that ensure property plays its part on the investment stage. They are used by investors and investment managers to:

- gauge property performance in different countries;
- uncover trends in key market sectors and segments;
- present overall statement of a country's investment property return;
- weigh up property returns with other assets and sectors
- forecast, and use as a basis for financial derivatives.

International Index Company

International Index Company (IIC) was established in 2001 as a joint venture between leading investment banks and major European exchange organisations. It is responsible for managing and administering the iBoxx, iTraxx credit derivative and iBoxx FX currency indices. IIC indices address the opacity and lack of standardised information in the FX, fixed income and credit derivative markets.

According to the company website, **www.indexco.com**, *"Fund managers rely on these indices for bond asset allocation and benchmarking; back offices value*

*see Chapter 4 for more information on GIPS.

portfolios with consolidated bond prices; fixed income research relies heavily on IIC's data for market analysis and to develop trading strategies."

IIC is headquartered in Frankfurt, Germany, and is owned by: ABN Amro, Barclays Capital, BNP Paribas, Deutsche BANK, Deutsche Börse, Dresdner Kleinwort, Goldman Sachs, HSBC, JP Morgan, Morgan Stanley and UBS.

Clearing Houses

What is a Clearing House?

A clearing house is an independent organisation, appointed by an exchange, which guarantees securities transactions. It completes the transactions on that exchange by seeing to validation, delivery and settlement. A clearing house may also offer novation, the substitution of a new contract or debt for an old, or other credit enhancement services to its members.

London Clearing House

The organisation, founded in 1888 to clear sugar and coffee trades in London, was originally known as the London Produce Clearing House. Once LCH has registered a trade, it becomes the buyer to every LCH member who sells and seller to every LCH member who buys, thereby guaranteeing that the financial obligations of trades are met.

The LCH clears trades conducted on the International Petroleum Exchange (IPE), the London International Financial Futures Exchange (LIFFE) incorporating the London Commodity Exchange (LCE), the London Stock Exchange and the London Metal Exchange (LME). It is owned by the major UK clearing banks (Barclays, Lloyds TSB, HSBC, Royal Bank of Scotland and Standard Chartered) and is a recognised clearing house under the regulatory supervision of the Financial Services Authority (FSA).

The London Clearing House Limited and Clearnet S.A. merged in 2004 to form the LCH.Clearnet Group. LCH.Clearnet will help achieve a widely sought-after goal – the consolidation of European Central Counterparty infrastructure, helping transform the efficiency and effectiveness of the EU's capital markets.

Settlement Banks

What is a Settlement Bank?

A settlement bank is a bank that provides settlement services to investment banks for their transactions.

Euroclear

Euroclear is the world's premier settlement system for domestic and international securities transactions, covering bonds, equities and investment funds.

Market owned and market governed, Euroclear provides securities services to major financial institutions located in more than 80 countries. In addition to its role as the leading International Central Securities Depositary (ICSD), Euroclear also acts as the Central Securities Depository (CSD) for Dutch, French, Irish and UK securities.

The Euroclear system clears a wide range of international fixed- and floating-rate paper, as well as domestic debt instruments. Participants are able to confirm, clear and settle in many currencies, on a delivery versus payment basis.

Euroclear owns the Crest settlement system, which along with settlement of fixed income instruments and funds provides a range of asset servicing and asset optimisation services, including full corporate actions facilities.

Clearstream

Clearstream Banking S.A. (CB) is the clearing division of Deutsche Börse, based in Luxembourg. It was created in January 2000 through the merger of Cedel International and Deutsche Börse Clearing, part of the Deutsche Börse Group which owns the Frankfurt Stock Exchange. Cedel, established in 1971, specialised in clearing and settlement. In 1996 it obtained a bank licence. In July 2002, Deutsche Börse purchased the remaining 50% of Clearstream International for €1.6 billion. Deutsche Börse's strategy is to be a vertical securities silo, providing facilities for the front and back ends of securities trading. By 2004, Clearstream contributed €114 million to Deutsche Börse's total Earnings Before Interest and Taxes (EBIT) of €452.6 million. It handled 50.0 million transactions and was custodian of securities worth €7,593 trillion.

The purpose of Clearstream is to facilitate money movements around the world, particularly by handling the resolution of sales of European stocks and bonds, in which market Clearstream was a major player, with an estimated 40% market share until May 2004 – together with its competitor Euroclear, the two firms settle 70% of European transactions.

DTCC

The Depository Trust & Clearing Corporation (DTCC) is a financial services company, based primarily at 55 Water Street in New York City, that provides clearance, settlement and information services for equities, corporate and municipal bonds, government and mortgage-backed securities, money market instruments and over-the-counter derivatives transactions.

DTCC was established in 1999 as a holding company for a group of operating companies providing securities clearance, settlement, and custody and information services.

Its depository custodies well over $25 trillion in stocks and bonds, more than any other depository in the world, and DTCC processes most of the securities transactions in the United States, over $1 quadrillion worth every year. DTCC was set up to provide an efficient and safe way for buyers and sellers of securities to make their exchange, and thus "clear and settle" transactions.

47

Trends in Investment Management

This chapter covers the trends that are shaping the investment management industry from the regulations introduced by regulators to the product ranges that are creating markets for the investment management firms.

Introduction

The investment management landscape is going through reform as new regulations and products are shaping the way firms do business. In the bid to increase profitability and remain competitive, investment management firms are not only reducing operating costs but are coming up with new products to generate more revenue and to stifle competition.

Regulatory compliance has been at the heart of investment management in recent times with the introduction of MiFID in Europe, Reg NMS in the US and also the third installation of UCITS, i.e. UCITS III. This is as a result of allegations of misconduct in the industry and the desire to raise regulatory standards.

In this section, the trends that are affecting the industry will be discussed and these include recently introduced directives as well as new products in the industry.

Introduction of MiFID

What is MiFID?

MiFID is the Markets in Financial Instruments Directive of the European Union. It contains 73 articles, applies to all investment firms in the EU and impacts on all asset classes except currency. MiFID is a directive that will replace the existing Investment Services Directive (ISD), the most significant European Union legislation for investment intermediaries and financial markets since 1995. MiFID is an integral part of the creation of a wider European market with liquidity to compete with the US.

The introduction of MiFID will promote market transparency and change the shape of sales distribution networks .Investment management firms will have to look at their cost base through a different lens than the one used one day.

Stated Aims of the European Union

The main objective of MiFID is to help issuers and investors by opening up markets and cutting the costs of securities trading. For example, investment management firms doing cross-border business will be affected by MiFID as it will simplify and streamline the passporting regime, increasing competition and enabling greater EU financial integration. These effects may act as catalysts for improved market efficiency.

The so-called concentration rule, which allows member states to give preference to regulated markets as distinct from other venues for the execution of securities transactions, will also be abolished in accordance with MiFID. Other aims of MiFID include setting a pan-European best execution obligation, which should enhance investor protection and price formulation, and allowing investment managers to realise the economic value of their trade data.

49

Impacts on Investment Management Firms

MiFID will impact on the following aspects of the investment management function:

- Order handling and best execution
- Transaction recording and record keeping
- Investor protection
- Pre- and post-trade transparency
- Conflicts of interest
- Outsourcing management
- Risk management
- Compliance
- Data management
- Investor administration
- Client communication

Impacts on IT in Investment Management

Investment management firms need to make IT changes in order to comply with MiFID and may well use this opportunity to go beyond their compliance obligations by identifying areas where technological innovation can support new business opportunities and get the best return on their IT investment. In addition, they could realise sustainable competitive advantage.

The detailed requirements for investment management vary from firm to firm but key changes may be either direct or indirect. Direct changes are those that are required to meet the letter of the law while indirect changes are those that, if effected early enough, may better prepare a firm to exploit the benefits of a new trading environment.

The following are changes that may be made by investment management firms:

- System internalisers[20] that execute trades between clients will most likely face the biggest challenge to implement the necessary network and data publishing infrastructure in time and will also be obliged to keep records with a view to displaying the same transparency that is currently required of exchanges.
- Investment management firms will be obliged to provide clear audit trails for transactions and show that they have met the new rules on "best execution".
- Investment firm that invested in algorithmic trading initiatives will need to create an over-arching framework to accommodate the MiFID programmes that may be underway.

20 Investment firms that, on an organised, frequent and systematic basis, deal on their account by executing client orders outside a regulated market or multilateral trading facility.

▓ As margin compression could potentially be the fallout from compliance with MiFID, investment management firms may have to compensate by creating new and innovative products to maintain their market position. A redesign of IT infrastructure will be required to support these new services and products quickly and competitively.

▓ Passporting of new activities will force a rethink on the outsourcing strategies in respect of the physical location of the key operations of the business.

Sarbanes-Oxley Act of 2002

The Sarbanes-Oxley Act of 2002 (known as Sox) was sponsored by US Senator Paul Sarbanes and US Representative Michael Oxley and it signifies the biggest change to federal securities laws in a long time. Large accounting scandals involving companies such as Enron, WorldCom, and Arthur Andersen, which resulted in billions of dollars in corporate and investor losses, instigated the changes to restore investor trust in the financial markets.

Since 2006, all public companies have been required to submit an annual assessment of the effectiveness of their internal financial auditing controls to the Securities and Exchange Commission (SEC). The types of companies affected include publicly traded companies in the United States, including all wholly owned subsidiaries, and all publicly traded non-US companies doing business in the US. Also included are private companies that are gearing up for an Initial Price Offering (IPO), which have to comply with certain aspects of the regulations.

There are 11 sections of the Sarbanes-Oxley Act, including sections 302, 401, 404 and 802. Section 404 – management of internal control – requires that financial reports must include an Internal Control Report stating that management is responsible for an "adequate" internal control structure. This is the most difficult section of the Act to comply with.

Non-compliance and submission of inaccurate certification could lead to a fine of $1 million and 10 years' imprisonment, even committed in error.

The Introduction of Hedge Fund Clones

A number of investment banks and financial services companies have launched hedge fund clones that could potentially lead to a shake-up of the $1,300bn hedge fund industry. The idea behind these clones is to undercut the relatively high fees that are charged by hedge fund managers.

There has been a widely accepted notion that there is substantial number of underperforming hedge fund managers in the industry and the high fees charged by the industry are unjustifiable. Industry experts believe that there is a lot of "dead wood" in the industry and that anyone can claim to be hedge fund manager. This has fuelled the speculation that these clones will be commonplace in the near future.

Hedge funds have traditionally based their strategies on generating the beta[21] of their chosen trading strategies without generating sufficient alpha[22] to justify their high fee structures. Hedge fund clones will be seeking to circumvent and exploit the deficiencies of these strategies with a view to offering returns on a par with those of hedge funds without the high fees to investors.

What is a Hedge Fund Clone?

Hedge fund clones are replication strategies that suggest hedge fund performance is largely driven by movements in underlying markets, such as equity, bond and commodity prices, rather than the inherent skill of managers. They are essentially funds designed to match the performance of existing successful funds by imitating their strategies.

Examples of recently launched Hedge Fund clones are as follows:

- **Merrill Lynch ML FX Clone** – a methodology for replicating hedge funds' foreign exchange (FX) strategies that will help investors to better understand and ultimately access the FX markets with greater ease and at lower cost.
- **Goldman's Absolute Return Tracker index (ART)** – based on the concept of decomposition of data derived from the performance characteristics of thousands of hedge funds with a view to calculating the aggregate position of the hedge fund universe.

Dow Jones Indexes already operates a suite of hedge fund indices that invest in a basket the managed accounts operated by hedge funds. However, it is understood that the company is of the opinion that the concept can be extended to create the same performance attributed by investing directly in the assets that hedge funds eventually invest in.

Growth of ETF Market

What are Exchange Traded Funds?

Exchange Traded Funds are funds that track an index, but can be traded like a stock. Investors can do just about anything with an ETF that they can do with a normal stock, such as short selling. ETFs have opened up new investment opportunities for private and institutional investors, offering an excellent means of achieving instant exposure to markets they want.

Exchange traded funds are evolving, with new products appearing across a broad range of asset classes. The market for ETFs continues to boom, with new

---

21 A measure of the correlation of movement between the price of an individual asset and market prices.
22 A measure of a manager's outperformance versus their benchmark.

products in new asset classes being listed across different exchanges. ETFs were launched in 1993 by Standard and Poor with the Standard and Poor's Deposit Receipt (SPDR, pronounced "Spider"). SPDRs gave investors an easy way to track the S&P 500 without buying an index fund, and they soon became quite popular. Ever since then, they have attracted interest from investors looking for a low-risk, cost-effective way of gaining exposure to a particular asset class.

Since the launch, the demand for ETFs has risen steadily to over €435 billion worldwide according to a Morgan Stanley report in February 2007 and the funds under management in ETFs are expected to exceed €1594bn (£1,083bn). The report also shows that the total number of ETFs was 730, with 1060 listings on 36 different exchanges, managed by 84 managers. There are also 516 ETFs to be listed in 2007.

The drivers behind this expected growth are as follows:

- A wider acceptance of these vehicles by institutional and retail investors.
- Larger allocation of funds to ETFs following regulatory changes in Europe and the US.
- Expansion in number and types of equity, fixed income and commodities indices.
- Plans from different exchanges to launch ETFs in the near future.

Market Segmentation

ETFs in Europe grew by 29.9% during the first half of 2006 compared to the 13.2% in US-listed ETFs, according to the Morgan Stanley report. Trading volumes increased 108.7% during the same period with an average daily trading volume of $34.3bn (£17.4bn) or 642.9m shares. The largest percentage increases were in Singapore, Hong Kong and Canada.

In the last few years there has been an increase in the influx of players into the ETF market but the market leader in terms of market share is Barclays Global Investors (BGI) which is well ahead of competitors. The figures below show the market segmentation.

Company	Assets Under Management (USD)	Market Share %
Barclays Global Investors	231.6	47.8
State Street Global Advisors	96.2	19.9
Others	156.5	32.3

In terms of products, BGI has a range of 166 ETFs, followed by Indexchange with 70.

Popularity of LDI

Liability Driven Investment (LDI) is currently a hot topic among those involved in managing pension assets. The current popularity of LDI is due in part to the opportunity it affords investors to reduce their portfolio risks. Investment managers believe the sector creates new commercial opportunities, allowing them to compete for a real role in liability matching.

Definition of LDI

Liability Driven Investing is a form of investing in which the main goal is to gain sufficient assets to meet all liabilities, both current and future. This form of investing is most prominent with defined-benefit pension plans, whose liabilities can often reach into the billions of dollars for the largest of plans. (www.investopedia.com)

It is a well-documented fact that institutional funds exist to support a stream of more-or-less committed cash outflows, or liabilities. This is evident in charities, insurance funds and pension funds. The same applies to retail funds aimed at providing for school fees or pension top-ups that have cash outflows to meet. The investment managers therefore use the assets of the fund to cover the liabilities of these funds over time rather than use them as an end in themselves to meet the expectations of their clients (insurance providers, trustees etc.). who are interested in the adequacy of the assets to match the liabilities and not the value of the assets in isolation.

Investment managers have always believed that management of liabilities was an actuarial role and have traditionally focused only on the asset side of the business. However in recent times the perception has changed dramatically, and increasingly investment managers are being asked to take responsibility for matching asset values to liabilities.

It can therefore be concluded that a Liability Driven Investment (LDI) strategy manages the assets of a fund relative to its liabilities. An LDI strategy effectively sets a risk budget so that assets closely match the liabilities of the fund in order to minimise the associated risks.

According to a Financial Times special report on LDI, there are five types of structures available. They are described as follows:

- The original structure, which involves a fund contracting with investment banks directly, taking on the role of counterparty and having risk-reducing derivative created solely for its liabilities.
- The second structure also gives pension funds access to bespoke swaps and hence better approximation to their required future income streams, but under an umbrella agreement with an investment manager.
- The remaining three structures are all pooled, i.e. funds in which multiple investors contribute assets and hold them as a group.

The following table[23] shows a range of both leveraged[24] and non-leveraged[25] LDI pooled products.

Fund Type	Description	Variants
Single Bullet	A small number of long-dated funds (typically 2 or 3) that each hold a zero coupon interest rate or inflation swap (bullet), paying out only at maturity (e.g. 20, 30 and 40-year swap funds)	Interest Rate Retail Price Index Limited Price Index
Multi-year "buckets"	A suite of funds, which themselves hold a series of annual zero coupon swaps. A common structure is to construct multiple 5-year buckets (e.g. a 2027–2031 fund paying out 5 equal annual cash flows over this time period, a 2032–2037 fund etc.)	Interest Rate Retail Price Index Limited Price Index
Year-on-Year	Numerous 1-year, zero coupon swap contracts, designed to meet a scheme's specific cash flows into the future.	Interest Rate Retail Price Index Limited Price Index

Investment Managers offer these products pre-packaged or otherwise.

Barclays Global Investors is currently the market leader in LDI across Europe, managing about £25bn worth.

Socially Responsible Investing

Ethical or socially responsible investment (SRI) involves considering the ethical, social and/or environmental performance of companies when selecting them for investment, as well as their financial performance. It is an area of investment management that means different things to different people; both veterans and newcomers alike. According to Eurosif, the European Social Investment Forum, "SRI combines investors' financial objectives with their concerns about social, environmental and ethical (SEE) issues." Many investors now include corporate governance (CG) matters along with SEE issues as part of the broader group of extra financial issues.

---

23 Information extracted from Financial Times Special Report on Liability Driven Investment 11/12/2006 pg 15 of FTfm.
24 The degree to which an investor or business is utilising borrowed money.
25 Operating without the use of borrowed money.

Socially responsible investing was once on the sidelines and a niche segment of investment management often viewed as the preserve of investors who value principles over profit. However, in recent times the perception has been changing rapidly as the SRI sector and mainstream begin to converge.

One of the main drivers for the promising shift to integrate SRI elements into investment strategies is climate change. Climate change poses not only an investment risk but also presents an opportunity for investors, owing to the rapid rate of growth in the clean technology sector that is estimated to be 30–50% a year. According to a Financial Times special report on Socially Responsible Investing, Goldman Sachs and Man Group are making big investments in the SRI sector by putting their own and clients' money into clean technology investments.

Eurosif categorises SRI into themes – "core SRI", which screens out companies, and more inclusive approaches it calls "broad SRI". The broad SRI market in the UK as at December 2005 was valued at €781 billion (£527.6 billion) while the core SRI market was valued at €30.5 billion (£20.6 billion).

Eurosif stated in a 2006 European SRI study that since 2003 the most significant area of development for SRI has been around improvements in integrating environmental, social and governance issues into investment decision-making. They identify the key factor as the creation of sell-side SRI teams and the resulting increase in financially oriented SRI investment research, which has built on the UK's strong position in Engagement companies on SRI issues and Core SRI practices.

The way an investment management firm approaches socially responsible investment depends on many different factors. These include the organisation's size, resources and motivations.

Investment managers need to meet the needs of their clients who are becoming more concerned about socially responsible investment issues, who in turn may be under pressure from concerned members and the general public. They may wish to use their institution's financial muscle and voice to influence the companies they choose to invest with, to ensure these companies have strategies for managing risk and reputation factors.

Ethical Investment Research Services (EIRIS) recognises this variety of factors and suggests three broad strategic approaches to SRI: screening, preference and engagement. Each of these approaches may be directed by the socially responsible criteria of the investor, in order to reflect their own particular concerns or areas of interest.

These strategies can be used individually or in combination. Passive fund management can also apply SRI principles by using SRI index tracking.

Screening

Screening is a strategy that involves creating a list of "acceptable" companies shaped by a combination of positive and/or negative factors. These may be companies whose conduct is viewed positively, such as those with good employment practices or those taking active steps to reduce levels of pollution. Or they may also be companies selected for avoiding involvement in certain negative practices or proscribed industries, such as tobacco production. This is a well-established strategy, particularly among retail funds, and it is popular with people who wish to make individual choices about what they do and do not want to invest in.

Preference
Preference requires the rating of companies according to a responsible investment policy. Fund managers apply the policy guidelines wherever possible, biasing investment decisions towards higher-rated companies. Fund managers select investments or portfolio weightings in them, taking into account how closely a company meets, or sets about meeting, the policy parameters. This method allows fund managers to integrate ethical with financial decision making; in cases where two companies get a similar rating against traditional financial indicators, you can compare them against your social, environmental, governance or other ethical indicators, and select the company with the better all-round performance.

Engagement
Engagement provides investors with an opportunity to influence corporate behaviour. It involves identifying companies that could improve their social, environmental, governance or other ethical policies and performance, and encouraging them along this path. This may be anything from writing an occasional letter of protest or support, to raising issues at the AGM or maintaining a detailed and direct dialogue with the company. At a basic level you could tell companies your policy and let them know how it affects your investment decision making or response to takeovers and share issues. A more developed engagement strategy would include persuading companies via regular meetings to improve their practices on issues such as product sourcing, recycling and pollution reduction. Another level of engagement is to offer to help companies formulate their own policy.

Socially Responsible Investment Index Trackers
Several SRI index tracker funds already exist. Within a given SRI approach, passive investment can be used to reduce management costs. It could also be used to seek out performance if you believe that a particular SRI approach identifies financially "better" investments. An SRI index tracker fund might mean a much narrower underlying list of stocks than conventional index trackers. Alternatively, "passive" techniques could reduce the variation in performance between an SRI universe of stocks and a conventional index.

A tracker approach can be used with screening or preference to track the universe of companies and may reduce management costs, whilst meeting other financial criteria. Computer-based approaches could adopt a variety of preference approaches – for example, adjusting the size of holdings according to overall SRI performance. It is also possible to use an SRI index to monitor your investment's performance according to SRI criteria if the criteria used for both are comparable.

Unit/ policy holder data from 1997

This is based on estimates provided by the SRI retail fund providers and the Investment Management Association. Note that fund providers are often only able to provide estimates.

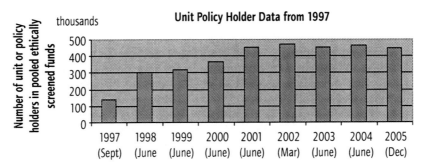

Source: EIRIS

According to Celent, SRI is a booming market in both the US and Europe with the European SRI market growing from €1 trillion in 2005 to €1.6 trillion in 2007.They predict that the SRI market in the US will reach $3 trillion by 2011.

Emergence of BRIC Investment Funds

The four largest emerging market countries are collectively known as BRIC, which stands for Brazil, Russia, India and China. BRIC is a relatively new buzz-word, mainly used in the investment world where a number of financial institutions are setting up so-called BRIC funds to give clients exposure to just these economies and stock markets.

The emergence of BRIC funds has been so rapid that critics no longer doubt that emerging markets are once more in vogue with investors of a certain profile; 2006 saw the launch of a number of BRIC funds by leading investment managers like Schroeder, Allianz, Goldman Sachs and Templeton. These funds normally seek growth by investing in companies listed in the BRIC markets and in companies with high exposure to those countries.

They are targeted at investors seeking access to those countries in particular. Many observers, though, believe specific focus on these countries should not be chosen over a focus on these countries in addition to similar countries experiencing similar growth. Despite the criticism, the performance figures paint a different picture for investors brave enough to take the plunge. According to Citywire, *"The UK market's sole onshore BRIC offering, the £32 million Allianz RCM BRIC Stars Fund, has made a return of 16.2% since it was launched at the end of February 2006. This compares to a mere 0.7% from the IMA's global emerging markets sector."*

Some Facts about "BRIC" Countries

- Combined they contain 43% of the world's population.
- Their economies hold real economic potential looking 5–20 years into the future, far more so than the west but with increased risk.
- India's economy grew by 6.9% in 2005 and is likely to become the third largest economy in the world behind the US and China.
- The Chinese economy could overtake both the UK and German economies in just five years.
- China is on course to deliver over 1 billion new consumers to the global economy over the next 25 years. (www.learnmoney.co.uk)
- Within 40 years the BRIC economies – which have a combined population of 2.7bn – could be larger than the G6 (original G7 countries minus Canada).
- The number of people in the BRIC countries with an annual income in excess of £1,750 per capita could double within three years.
- Between 2000 and 2005, BRIC contributed 28% of global economic growth.
- As of late 2005, their share of global trade reached 15%, they held more than 30% of the world's foreign exchange reserves and accounted for 18% of oil demand.
- The collective size of the BRIC stock markets could almost reach that of the US, UK, Germany and Russia by 2050.
- Some companies in the BRIC countries are now a force to be reckoned with in their respective industry sectors. Notable examples are Gazprom in Russia, which is the fifth largest company in the world, and ICBC in China with a market capitalisation of close to $170 billion. These are indicators of the potential importance of these countries in the global equity markets.

Downside to Investing in BRIC Funds

- Vulnerability to currency movements, for example the massive devaluation in the rouble in 1998 after the Russian government defaulted on its debt payments.
- Investing in BRIC funds gives limited exposure to the wider opportunities available in emerging markets, especially in countries like Taiwan and Thailand.
- BRIC Funds often focus closely on the countries' indices rather than the best stock opportunities.
- Slow-down in consumer spending in BRIC economies could hit BRIC Funds.

Flow of Funds to Gulf States

Countries such as Qatar, Kuwait, Saudi Arabia, Bahrain and Oman in the Middle East are referred to as Gulf States. The economies of countries in these regions have enjoyed strong economic growth since 2003. According to Middle East North Africa Financial Network (MENAFN), "Real GDP growth for the region was

8.5% in 2003, 5.9% in 2004, 6.8% in 2005 and an estimated 6% in 2006, and is forecast to grow at a healthy 5.0% in 2007." The following figures were recorded for economic growth for the individual countries in the region:

- UAE – 10.2%
- Qatar – 7.5%
- Kuwait – 6.5%
- Saudi Arabia – 6.2%
- Bahrain – 6%
- Oman – 5%

Given the healthy real GDP growth shown above, it is no surprise that western asset managers and UK pension funds have finally begun investing in the equity markets of the fast-growing Middle East. According to industry watchers, western institutional investors began to show interest in the region in 2005 as the petro-dollar boom sent Gulf equity markets spinning to record highs.

They also noticed that foreign inflows really took off after the stock market correction in the first quarter of 2006, representing the steepest sell-offs in emerging market history, pushing valuations back to more realistic levels. Prior to this and up to 2004, the majority of the money coming in was purely regional. In 2005, foreign investors woke up to the situation and the correction generated significant foreign interest.

Interests of western countries in the equity markets of the Gulf regions are underscored by the launch in 2006 of the investible index based on the Dubai stock exchange by Merrill Lynch, allowing investors to sidestep restrictions on direct foreign ownership of equities.

Popularity of Property Funds

Property funds are funds that invest in commercial property, such as industrial property, warehouse buildings, shopping units and office blocks. As stated in Chapter 1, property is an asset class in its own right, but it performs differently from other asset classes such as equities and bonds and should be considered as part of any balanced portfolio to improve diversification.

Commercial property should not be confused with residential property, as they are two distinct categories. Residential property is subject to emotional issues and the current valuation of UK residential property is not matched by the rental incomes that can be achieved. On the other hand, commercial property is able to generate rental income which is subject to upward-only reviews.

Commercial property funds have become increasingly popular with both institutional and private investors. This growth in popularity is largely due to the outstanding returns they have provided and the diversification they offer away from equities and bonds. Over five years to the end of 2005, according to the Investment Property Databank index, commercial property comfortably outperformed equities and bonds, returning 85.8%, compared with 11.6% (FTSE All Share) and 33.6% (gilts).

Variants of property funds include property fund of funds and property derivatives. Property fund of funds are funds that invest in other property funds to achieve even greater diversification than traditional property funds, while property derivatives provides an alternative method of investing in commercial property without having to buy or sell the physical assets.

Popularity of property fund of funds is due largely to the attempt to redefine property as an actively managed asset class almost like listed equity. Investment managers in the property sector are of the opinion that allocations can be shifted from country to country and even sectors such as offices and retail.

As for property derivatives, they are gaining traction in the financial marketplace owing to the fact that property is one of the last major asset classes in the Western markets without a liquid derivatives market behind it. Whilst the market for property derivatives is in its infancy, the market size in the UK is estimated to approach £3 trillion[26] over the next few years.

Popularity of 130/30 Investment Strategy

Investors who seek better performance have traditionally sought managers who can provide better returns than a benchmark index. However, in recent years the framework has been expanded as investors get more sophisticated .Many of these investors consider alternatives that can provide higher risk-adjusted returns. Their objective is to realise greater benefits from their investment manager's skills in producing attractive performance, albeit within specific risk tolerances, that gives them better flexibility to implement their ideas.

To this end, a new portfolio structure has been devised. This is known in the industry as 130/30, active extension or limited shorting. It is investment management's latest "big idea" and it is a strategy designed to produce higher returns than a typical long-only strategy. Industry experts believe that the logic behind it is flawless, which explains why it has gained favour with plan sponsors and is moving into the retail investment mainstream.

A 130/30 strategy is considered a lucrative option for investors who want the benefit of shorting without committing assets to a market-neutral strategy. The strategy is relatively straightforward and the following is an illustration of the concept:

- The investment manager invests £100 in stocks.
- They borrow stocks and sell them short, generating £30.

26 Rothery, Andrew. "Why the success of property derivatives is far from certain" *Finance Week* 2 March, 2005: 17.

▓ They spend that £30 on more stocks.
▓ The net result is a portfolio that is 130% long and 30% short.

It should be noted that whilst 130/30 is a typical portfolio structure, the investment strategy can be modified to 110/10, 120/20 or another variation that suits the investor's specific requirements and results in a net investment of 100%. Nevertheless, "130/30" is the established industry vocabulary.

The growing importance of the "130/30" strategy has been highlighted in a prediction by leading investment bank Merrill Lynch that these strategies will be an important feature of the investment landscape during 2007. Merrill Lynch also estimates that around $50 billion of pension fund money globally is already invested in 130/30s. According to Citywire "the vast majority so far is in quant funds, which invest according to predefined, purely quantitative criteria. Leading providers include quant giants such as State Street, Mellon and BGI."

The Introduction of the Revised Investment Performance Standards

The Investment Management industry requires transparency and discipline in the reporting of performance, an area that is perceived as being far too opaque. In order to address this issue, an investment performance standard needs to be in place for the benefit of the client and the industry as a whole, adopted on a worldwide basis. This led to the introduction of GIPS.

What are GIPS?

Global Investment Performance Standards (GIPS) are a set of standards for the presentation of investment manager performance, endorsed by a total of 26 countries. They can also be defined as a set of ethical principles used by investment management firms in order to establish a globally standardised, industry-wide approach to creating performance presentations that communicate investment results to prospective clients. GIPS were introduced in 1999 but a revised version was approved on 4 February 2005 by the CFA Institute Board of Governors. The CFA Institute created and administers the GIPS standards through a GIPS secretariat and partners with local country sponsors in the 26 countries to promote the standards.

Since 1 January 2006, which was the effective date for the revised standards, GIPS have moved away from allowing variations in national standards, which took account of local country circumstances, to the adoption of a uniform or "gold" standard. All presentations that include performance results for periods after 31 December 2005 must meet all the requirements of the revised GIPS standards.

There are five main sections of GIPS that reflect the basic elements and cover the following:

- The choice of input data;
- Calculation methodology;
- Composite[27] construction;
- Disclosures;
- Presentation and Reporting Methods.

These represent a guideline for investment managers in accordance with requirements laid down by the UK Financial Services Authority and also for compliance with GIPS.

GIPS are truly global standards and investment management firms operating in the global markets need to comply for the following reasons:

- There is increasing globalisation of financial markets and investment management firms, hence the globalisation of the investment process and exponential growth of assets under management.
- The standardisation of investment performance measurement and presentation recognisable worldwide will be beneficial to prospective clients.
- Investors are assured of a performance presentation standard that is both complete and fairly presented.
- A global investment performance standard is in place that gives prospective and existing clients a greater degree of confidence in the performance numbers presented by investment management firms.

Countries that endorse the GIPS Standard
The following are countries that are sponsors of the GIPS standard:

- Australia
- Austria
- Belgium
- Canada
- Denmark
- France
- Germany
- Hong Kong
- Hungary
- Ireland
- Italy
- Japan
- Liechtenstein
- Luxembourg
- Micronesia
- Netherlands
- New Zealand

---

27 A composite is an aggregation of several portfolios managed in similar way.

- Norway
- Portugal
- Singapore
- Spain
- South Africa
- Sweden
- Switzerland
- United Kingdom
- United States

UCITS III Regulations[28]

Background
The original UCITS directive (Undertakings for Collective Investment in Transferable Securities) was enacted by the European Union in 1985. Its objective was to enable uniform regulation of retail investment funds across Member States and allow cross-border marketing and distribution of funds throughout the EU.

However, the original UCITS did not fully achieve this goal as constraints in the definition of eligible investments restricted the market potential of UCITS funds. In addition, each Member State created individual rules which created obstacles to cross-border marketing.

A revised set of directives, UCITS III, were enacted in January 2002 and implemented through 2007 in two parts.

Management Directive
This enabled a "European passport" for investment managers to operate throughout the EU and widened the activities which they are allowed to undertake by defining control mechanisms for the protection of retail investors. These included the requirement for a simplified prospectus to be provided to investors.

Product Directive
This widened the scope of investment objectives for an UCITS fund, enabling investments in money market instruments, derivatives, index-tracking funds and funds of funds, and allowing asset classes to be mixed in one fund.

Eligible Assets
After a lengthy consultation process, CESR (Committee of European Securities Regulators) published guidelines concerning the eligible assets allowed for investment by UCITS in March 2007. These were designed to ensure a uniform interpretation of the UCITS directive and include:

28 Contributed by Michael Harriman of Positive View Ltd.

- ■ Article 2   Transferable securities (incl. Embedded derivatives)
- ■ Articles 3–7   Money market instruments
- ■ Article 8   Financial derivative instruments
- ■ Article 9   Financial indices
- ■ Article 10   Securities which embed derivatives
- ■ Article 11   Efficient Portfolio Management
- ■ Article 12   Index replicating UCITS

Derivatives

A significant impact of UCITS III is the ability to use derivatives for investment purposes, i.e. to increase the investment return and enable innovative products, rather than purely for the purpose of hedging, reducing risk and/or costs. This enables UCITS managers to adopt many of the investment characteristics of higher risk, higher return hedge funds including a wider use of OTC and credit derivative instruments.

Credit derivatives are derivatives which transfer the credit risk of an underlying instrument from one party to another without transferring the instrument itself e.g. Credit Default Swaps.

UCITS III requires that exposure to derivative instruments does not exceed 100% of the net asset value of the overall fund. The interpretation of exposure varies between the regulatory authorities of each Member State. However, the principle of the directive is that a formal risk management process is required which is proportionate to the complexity and the sophistication of derivatives within the fund.

Commitment Approach

For a "non-sophisticated" UCITS fund, the derivative exposure can be measured through a "commitment approach" whereby the exposure is calculated from the nominal value of the underlying instrument(s).

Value at Risk

A "sophisticated" UCITS fund generally requires Value at Risk (VaR) monitoring supplemented by stress testing and scenario analysis. VaR measures the historical volatility and covariance of a fund's assets and calculates the maximum loss that could be expected in a given period with a given level of confidence (e.g. 99%).

EU guidelines do not clearly define a "sophisticated" UCITS, which leads to differences of interpretation between Member States. The general principle implies that more sophisticated investment strategies require sophisticated risk management procedures (i.e. VaR).

Principles-based Regulation

In the UK, UCITS III has been implemented by the FSA within the New Collective Investment Schemes sourcebook (COLL) and all UCITS funds were required to convert to UCITS III by 28 February 2007.

The FSA has pressed for eligibility of assets within UCITS III funds to be

65

judged on a principles basis as part of its overall drive towards "Principles-based Regulation". The balance of the FSA Handbook and the FSA approach to supervision will rely increasingly on principles and outcome-focused rules rather than detailed rules prescribing how outcomes must be achieved.

This increases the flexibility and the scope for UCITS managers to innovate; however the impact of such regulation is to:

- increase focus on the quality of the investment management decision;
- impose fewer restrictions on investment instruments, with less prescriptive rules but increased monitoring, fiduciary control and risk management requirements;
- extend the range of instruments and new fund products requiring flexibility of systems and processes to enable timely introduction of new instruments;
- intensify the need for quality and depth of data which creates pressure on firms to focus on data management;
- expand the number of regulatory guidelines, which will require firms to adapt their business processes and controls.

Implications of UCITS III on Information Technology

Investment firms face an increasing change in the culture of compliance across the enterprise and an increased demand for transparency in the investment process to conform to the principles-based regulatory environment introduced with UCITS III.

There are impacts on IT systems across the enterprise including: Front office, Trading, Data Management, Portfolio Valuation, Risk Management, Client Reporting, Performance Measurement and Compliance.

Key provisions include the following.

Full Instrument Coverage

While the focus of automation has traditionally been on purpose-built front-office systems, the increased use of OTC derivatives has initiated a shift in focus towards the automation of alternative assets in the middle and back office.

Valuation and Reconciliation

Portfolio accounting systems must be able to ensure a reliable and timely valuation on a daily basis. Processes must be in place to calculate derivative exposure and enable reconciliation of OTC positions.

Investment Risk monitoring

"Sophisticated" UCITS III funds require sophisticated risk processes and controls including VaR monitoring tools with stress testing and scenario analysis support.

Comprehensive Data Management support

IT systems must have the capability of recording, processing and controlling an expanding range of asset classes with variable data attributes, contractual obligations and processing requirements.

Structured products, including Asset Backed Securities, Credit-linked Notes and Collateralised Debt Obligations (CDOs) should be able to be decomposed to their constituent components and underlying instruments.

Document Management

A direct consequence of the move towards principles-based regulation is the weight regulators place on the fund documentation and internal controls rather than conformance with a prescriptive regulator rule set. Electronic document management solutions reduce operational costs and reduce human error, assisting investment firms to achieve this goal.

Compliance Monitoring and Incident Resolution Workflow

Of critical importance in monitoring UCITS III funds is the ability of pre-trade and post-trade compliance monitoring tools to adapt to new asset classes and the variable rules required for principles-based regulation. Integration with a variety of IT solutions is critical. Incident Resolution management is required to enable transparency of the monitoring process and regulatory review.

Flexible Solutions

The primary challenge facing Information Technology in supporting UCITS III funds and the new principles-based regulatory environment is the ability to adapt.

The overriding requirement is flexibility in the design and configuration of systems and procedures to adapt to new regulations, guidelines and interpretations.

Growth of Islamic Asset Management

The recent focus of the investment world on the burgeoning Islamic asset management market was borne out of the demand for Shari'a-compliant investment funds, i.e. funds that are invested in accordance with Shari'a principles. Islamic investment funds are not new to the market, in fact they have been around since the late 1980s. However, in recent times the marketplace for these funds has been maturing and growing and it is difficult to think of any major financial institution that has not participated in the promotion of an investment fund.

Despite the establishment of the first Islamic investment fund in the late 1980s, the real catalyst to the development of these funds was a ruling by the Fiqh Academy of the Organisation of Islamic Countries which required that "shares" in a company were defined as an "undivided portion of the company's assets". Prior to this, the idea of whether investing in shares (or equities) was allowable under Shari'a law was debatable. The ruling, however, presented an opportunity to millions of Muslims throughout the world that were looking to invest their surplus earning or savings in this sector in agreement with Shari'a Law.

Definition

Islamic asset management can be defined as the professional management of collective investments in different types of assets based on the principles of Shari'a and guided by Islamic economics.

Islamic investment funds can therefore be defined as investment vehicles permissible by Shari'a law and managed on the basis of Mudaraba or agency contract.

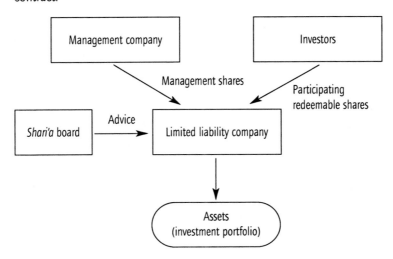

According to one estimate, the Islamic finance industry has assets worth over $US750 billion and is considered one of the fastest growing industries in the world.

Introduction of IAS 39

International Accounting Standard 39: Financial Instruments: Recognition and Measurement (IAS 39) is one of the accounting standards that must be complied with for companies reporting under International Financial Reporting Standards (IFRS). It defines the valuation and reporting of financial instruments, such as derivatives, loans and employee option schemes.

Basically, IAS 39 requires changes to the value of financial assets to have a profit and loss effect, and it defines valuation techniques. Financial instruments used for hedging, as strictly defined in the standard, are exempt from a P&L effect under normal circumstances. IAS 39 is a long and controversial standard which attempts to regulate in detail an area of innovation in corporate finance, so interpretation and application of the standard will prove difficult. IAS 39 is heavily influenced by the work of United States' accounting standard setters. IAS 39 also advances the accounting profession's attack on historical value as the basis for balance sheet valuation.

Impact of IAS 39 on Investment Managers

Investment managers are increasingly faced with compliance with IAS39 and this is more evident in the recent growth of the Exchange Traded Funds market. This has led to the development of investment strategies in the shape of ETFs to comply with transparency and liquidity rules in some countries.

The Emergence of Currency as an Asset Class in Investment Management

In recent times, currencies as an asset class have moved into the limelight from the speculative fringe into the mainstream of institutional investment management. The reason for this emergence is that currency portfolios are perceived to compare favourably against others in terms of return, risk and correlation statistics. In addition to this, institutional investors are increasingly hungry for alpha (or excess returns) and are looking beyond the traditional asset classes.

Currencies stand out as an asset class of choice for the following reasons:

■ The global foreign exchange (FX) market is considered as by far the largest marketplace in the world both geographically and in terms of trading volumes.
■ FX markets, unlike other markets, allow investment managers to analyse their reciprocal values. A falling US dollars/Euro is synonymous with a rising Euro because the US dollars can be expressed in Euro, and vice versa.
■ The reciprocity inherent in currency pairing makes the expression "short sale" – maligned in equity trading – non-existent in currency trading because the short sale of a currency is equivalent to a purchase of the other currency.
■ Currency markets are also unique in the sense that they are active without interruption "round-the-clock".
■ Currency markets are largely inefficient and as a result can provide significant returns.

There is little doubt that asset money has been flowing into the currency sector albeit slowly. According to the Financial Times, currency managers have been expanding their client list in recent times .Many of these new clients have signed up for absolute return mandates, confirming their hopes that currencies represent a tradable asset and not just a hedgeable risk.

Exploring the Potential of Exchange Traded Commodities for UCITS[29]

Investors have been demanding exposure to commodities for a number of years but until recently, UCITS funds would gain exposure to commodities through

---

29 Contributed by Nik Bienkowski, CFA of ETF Securities.

purchasing commodity companies (equities) or commodity funds as there were no other eligible alternatives. With the progress of financial innovation over the past 20 years since the first UCITS directive was released, new eligible investments exist for UCITS investment managers which are a "direct" investment in commodities rather than an indirect investment.

Direct versus indirect commodities investment

Until recently, there was no way to gain direct exposure to commodities unless you were a sophisticated investor. Ordinary investors could only gain indirect exposure through resources companies (e.g. BP, Rio Tinto) and commodity funds. It is important to understand the differences between direct exposure such as Exchange Traded Commodities (ETCs) and indirect exposure:

- **Exposure to commodity prices** – ETCs are perfectly correlated with the underlying commodity, commodity companies are not.
- **An investment in management** – An investment in commodity companies is an investment in management (equities), which so happens to operate within the commodity space.
- **Correlation and portfolio performance** – ETCs have lower correlation to equities than do commodity companies, which results in superior portfolio performance.
- **Current state of the industry** – Industry fundamentals such as rising costs and falling reserves can be negative for commodity companies while positive for the underlying commodity.

Development of the UCITS directive and commodity markets

When the first UCITS directive was being created at the start of the 1980s, commodity markets existed but in a much different form from today. They were also the realm of producers and "sophisticated" institutional investors only. Today, commodities markets have become regulated, transparent, liquid and large markets. In addition, new financial innovations have resulted in simple, safe and secure exchange-traded securities.

Typical Features

	1986	2006
Portfolio Composition	Bonds, equities	Bonds, equities, real-estate, alternatives (hedge funds, commodities)
Oil market	90% of oil was sold under long-term bespoke forward contracts between industry players	Most liquid commodity markets in the world
	Oil futures only began in 1983	Notional volume exceeds US$40bn/day

70

	Traded in the pit for a few hours a day between a limited number of traders	Markets are regulated
		Moving to 100% electronic trading
	Pricing was opaque and illiquid	Benchmarks are liquid and transparent
Gold investment	Investment was made via physical bars or certificates representing physical bars, redeemable in gold	ETFs, ETCs and structured products
		Transparent benchmarks and pricing
	Gold was not a traded security	
		Listed on regulated markets
UCITS & commodities	Indirect exposure allowed via commodity companies (like Shell)	Transferable securities allowed
		Exchange Traded Commodities (ETCs)
	Managed funds allowed	
	No holding of precious metals or certificates representing them	

Exchange Traded Commodities

Exchange Traded Commodities (ETCs) are similar to Exchange Traded Funds (ETFs). They enable ordinary investors to buy and sell exposure to commodities through regular brokerage accounts, providing cheap and easy access to an asset class (or sector) that has previously been difficult to access. ETCs trade and settle like equities (e.g. CREST T+3), are listed on major stock exchanges and have all the same order types as equities, such as limit orders and shorts. ETCs are simple, unleveraged, perpetual investments (non-expiring) which track the world's largest commodity markets. ETCs can be used as a strategic or tactical tool for any portfolio or investor.

Overview of Portfolio Management and Administration

This chapter gives an overview of portfolio management and the administration of portfolios in line with investors' requirements and investment managers' styles and philosophies.

Introduction

In investment management, there is no right or wrong way to manage clients' investments as individual investment managers have their own preferred style of portfolio management based on their concept of economic theory.

What is common to all investment managers, however, is their obligation to the investors and beneficiaries of the portfolio of funds under management, which is fulfilled by striking the requisite balance between risk and reward and operating within the confines of the applicable constitutional and regulatory requirements.

Definitions of Portfolio Management
1. The art and science of making decisions about investment mix and policy, matching investments to objectives, asset allocation for individuals and institutions, and balancing risk vs. performance. (Investopedia)
2. The process of managing the assets of a mutual fund, including choosing and monitoring appropriate investments and allocating funds accordingly. (Investorwords)

Portfolio management in investment management should not be confused with "IT Portfolio Management" which is an about managing resources for IT projects and programmes.

Investor Requirements

Investors make investments to make returns. However, investors have individual reasons for committing to an investment at different times. What is common to all investors is the need for income or a future capital sum and the balance between risk and reward.

The attitudes of investors towards religion, financial security and ethics are some of the factors that shape their investment criteria and the investment manager advises the investor on this basis when selecting a fund. Investors also factor in tax considerations when weighing up alternative investment vehicles.

Investment managers manage clients' expectation when recommending a fund to ensure that the investors are aware of the realistic boundaries of the return on their investments.

Asset Allocation

As mentioned in Chapter 1, the different asset classes – equities, bonds, real estate, cash and currency – are the central focus of asset allocation. The exercise of allocating funds among these assets (and among individual securities within each asset class) is what investment management firms are paid for.

Asset classes have their unique characteristics in respect of market dynamics and interaction effects and hence influence the allocation of monies to obtain the best performance for the fund. In this exercise, the fund is first apportioned between the different asset classes, different geographical locations (e.g. US, Europe and the Far East) and different sectors (e.g. retail, telecoms and pharmaceuticals). It could be argued that the performance of a fund is dependent on the skills of the investment manager in constructing the asset allocation and completing it with individual asset holdings with a view to outperforming identified benchmarks. The allocation weightings are adjusted from time to time to accommodate vagaries of the markets as indicated in economic and market forecasts.

Investment managers that operate an asset allocation process are often referred to as *top-down* investment managers. Those that operate an opposite methodology – *bottom-down*, whereby stock selection precedes building of the funds – are known as bottom-down investment managers.

Example of Asset Allocation

The asset allocation working group of Biz Global Investors has decided to increase the allocation in the Japanese Markets for the next year. The benchmark weighting is 30%. This implies that the Japanese equity market is 30% market capitalisation of the global index at present. The working group increases the proportion of the fund's assets to be invested in Japan to 40%. The constitution of the fund with regard to stock is the prerogative of the working group that specialises in Japanese equities.

Stock Selection

Stock selection is an art that has been perfected by investment managers over the years. When selecting stocks for a portfolio, the investment managers consider the following key issues amongst others:

- downward or upward price movements of a selection of stocks;
- performance of a given industry sector;
- individual investment philosophy;
- determination of a stop-loss;
- risk–reward trade-offs;
- news and announcements.

Investment Styles

In investment management, there are two strategies that investment managers adopt in managing their portfolios: passive and active management. There are differing opinions about which strategy is most advisable to adopt in light of the quest for performance of funds.

Active Management

The following is a definition of active management from Investopedia:

> *"An investing strategy that seeks returns in excess of a specified benchmark."*

Active Management is the art of stock picking and market timing. In an ideal scenario, the manager exploits inefficiencies in the financial markets by buying undervalued securities and selling short the securities that are overvalued. Investment managers use active management to achieve a goal of less volatility or risk than the benchmark index instead of greater long-term return depending on the specific investment portfolio.

Active portfolio managers use a variety of factors and strategies to construct their portfolios. These include measures such Price/Earning (P/E) ratios and sector bets that attempt to anticipate long-term macroeconomic trends.

It should be noted that the performance of an actively managed investment portfolio depends on the skills of the manager and the research analysts that provide market information. Industry experts are of the opinion that most actively managed collective investment schemes, i.e. funds, hardly ever outperform their index opposite number over a sustained period of time, assuming that they are benchmarked correctly.

Active management differ from passive management (see below) where the investment manager does not seek to "beat" the benchmark index.

Advantages of Active Management

Investment managers and investors are attracted to active management largely because it permits the selection of investments that are not representative of the market in general. However, investors have different reasons for committing to investments and the following could be advantages of active management:

- Investors that are risk averse and want less volatility may want investment in less risky, high-quality companies as opposed to the market as a whole. This may mean that they will accept slightly lower margins.
- On the other hand, it is attractive to investors who want returns higher than the market returns and are less risk averse.
- Not all investors believe in the efficient markets hypothesis (see passive management below).
- The diversification offered by investments that are out-of-step with the market.

Disadvantages of Active Management

- Associated fees and transaction costs are higher than those in passive management.
- As the asset base of an actively managed fund gets to a certain size, it gradually assumes index-like characteristics because it must invest in an increasingly diverse set of investments instead of only those that represent the fund manager's initiative.

Passive Management

Passive management (also called passive investing) refers to a buy-and-hold approach to money management. It is a financial strategy in which an investment manager makes as few portfolio decisions as possible with a view to minimising transactions, including incurring capital gains tax. Investment managers are drawn to passive management because it is a popular method that mimics the performance of an externally specified index – called "index funds".

Passive management is most commonly used in the equity market where index funds track stock market indices. However, in recent times it is increasingly used in other asset classes, including bonds and real estate. As seen in Chapter 2, there is a wide variety of market indexes around the world and many index funds track a number of them.

The market leaders in investment management, including Barclays Global Investors and State Street, practise this form of money management.

Reasons for Choosing this Strategy

The following are theoretical concepts of economics that underpin passive management:

- Efficient Market Hypothesis – which postulates that markets are broadly efficient in the sense that information is freely available, making it almost impossible to outperform the market.
- Capital Asset Pricing Model (CAPM) – which essentially postulates that the total risk on a portfolio, as measured by the variation in its returns, is less than the weighted average risk of the constituent securities.
- The principal–agent problem – this problem is borne out of the assessment of the incentives that a principal (investor), who allocates money to an investment manager (the agent), must give the manager to ensure that the portfolio is run in line with the investor's risk/reward appetite and the monitoring of the agent's performance.

How do Investment Managers implement Passive Investing?

As seen in Chapter 2, index funds are funds that track the performance of the stock market index. They are implemented by purchasing securities in the same proportions as the stock market index or by sampling, i.e. buying stocks of each kind and sector in the index or, in a more sophisticated way, buying shares that have the best chance of good performance.

Investment advisors invest passively for their clients in a globally diversified portfolio of index funds.

Portfolio Administration

Having discussed the salient points about portfolio management in the last section, it is necessary to understand the administrative elements that support the management processes.

Portfolio administration is an essential aspect of the investment management process and one that is prone to errors. It is an area where mistakes could lead to regulatory breaches, which could prove costly to the organisation.

The following are the key elements of portfolio administration.

Best Execution

Best execution is about buying and selling securities, i.e. trading. In order to ensure best execution, the fund manager must get the optimum bid or offer price for the type and size of trades.

Buying and selling can be done either on an agency basis, which attracts a commission because it is routed to a broker, or a principal basis. In either case, buying of shares in the UK will incur stamp duty, i.e. tax.

Settlement and Delivery

Settlement and delivery are the procedures for delivering the stocks that are sold and the payment of cash for those that are bought for the fund under management. Settlement and delivery procedures in portfolio administration are dependent on the nature of the market in respect of the obligations of the respective counterparties in a trade and the rules of the market. With the advent of straight-through processing, settlement and delivery procedures are automated, with the terms of the settlement and delivery defined in the business rules of the settlement system.

In the case of pension funds and unit trusts, it is the trustee that is responsible for settlement as registered legal owner of the security in the fund. As for OEICs, it is the responsibility of the custodian.

Registration

Registration is essentially about ensuring that the securities that make up a fund are duly registered to provide evidence of legal title to these securities. When a company issues a stock or share, the details of the share are entered into a stock register that is maintained by the company or its registrars. The details of the legal owner, especially the name, should match that of the legal owner of the stock, which could be the trustee or the custodian.

When trades are executed, the registration details are electronically transferred to the company's registrar; although this can be done manually via a stock transfer form, the electronic medium is preferred in most organisations. An essential item in the details is the registration date.

The registration date is essential in the entry because it shows the date the fund becomes the legal owner of the securities. This is the date that the ownership commences and the full rights – which include rights to vote and attend meetings – to the security take effect. This date will also be used to determine the dividend or interest payments.

Custody

In Chapter 1, custody was described as a financial institution that has the legal responsibility for a customer's securities. What is essential in portfolio administration is the reconciliation of records (on the security) between the fund manager and the custodian.

There are custodians called depositories that are legal owners or registered holders of non-domiciled securities.

Use of Nominees

The use of nominees in portfolio administration is mainly used for achieving a certain level of efficiency. Nominees, as the name implies, are organisations that act as proxies for other organisations. However, in the context of investments, a nominee is the name on the register in place of the legal owner.

The benefits of using a nominee are as follows:

- It eliminates the need to transfer the title to trust property whenever there are changes in the trustee body.
- It facilitates the transfer of trust property into, and out of, the trust (for example, when shares are bought and sold).
- It reduces the risk of trust documents, evidencing the title to the trust property, being lost.

An illustration of the use of nominees is as follows:

BigFund Bank is the trustee of the Biz Common Investment Fund; the fund's assets are registered naming the owner as BigFund Bank, but ensuring that there is an obvious link to the fund. The fund was therefore named "Bigfund Nominee Subaccount BizCIF".

Records and Regulation

Fund managers have to keep records to provide evidence that they have carried out their business in an efficient and compliant manner. Records to be kept include:

- settlement
- dividend and interest entitlements
- rights and bonus issues, capital reconstructions and takeovers
- dividend reinvestment
- capital gains tax calculations
- corporate actions such as name changes, reconstructions, spin-offs and consolidations.

These records must be held for at least three years or longer and be accessible for inspection by regulators and trustees.

Portfolio Accounting and Controls

A key aspect of fund administration is accounting of transactions and keeping accurate records of these transactions. Equally important is the control of the portfolio's activities to ensure compliance with the specifications of the fund, i.e. objectives and policies, as stated in the documentation of the fund to investors.

Activities involved in portfolio accounting include:

▉ maintenance of investment accounts which separate capital transactions from income transactions and provide statements of realised and unrealised profit and losses(PnL); also included in the statements are assets and cash inflows and outflows and current and comparative positions and valuations;
▉ analyses and projections for the tracking and adjustment of fund performance in terms of yield and distribution targets;
▉ accounting for the management company which involves collating data on the dealings in the units/shares of the funds and income from initial, exit and annual charges less discounts and commissions.

As for the controls, activities will include:

▉ regular reconciliations of records with banks and custodians in respect of cash and stock positions of the fund's capital accounts;
▉ reconciliation of dividend and interest income in the income account;
▉ clearance of outstanding and mismatching items or amounts;
▉ evaluation of the effectiveness of accounting functions through routine compliance monitoring and audits.

With appropriate procedures and processes in place, the investment management firm can provide evidence of best practices in accounting and operations and also adherence to each fund's stated objectives and investment policies.

Profits, income and taxation

As shown in the "records and regulations" section above, complete and accurate records should be kept for profits, income and taxation.

Realised and unrealised profits and losses are created in the capital account by portfolio transactions. Revaluations (marking to market) of individual assets in the portfolio generate unrealised profits and losses, i.e. for values in the local currency. For foreign securities revaluation will also involve conversion of the value of the asset and as well as cash into the local currency.

The income aspect of fund administration involves the following:

▉ collection of income on investments and interest on uninvested cash, along with any fees or commissions earned;
▉ payment of expenses, charges and taxes;
▉ recording of income to verify that all entitlements are received;
▉ payment of permitted expenses;
▉ net income allocation and distribution to individual unit/shareholder;
▉ reporting on income to the appropriate tax authorities, for example HM Revenue and Customs, as required.

As for taxation, there is no standard procedure as there are variations in accordance with the type of fund and jurisdiction. In most cases, funds are treated as companies that carry on the business of investment holding and, as such, tax is only paid on income accrued from dividend, interest etc. allowing for expenses of management.

The details of taxation as it applies to funds and jurisdictions are out of the scope of this book. Readers are advised to consult other specialist publications on tax and investment/fund management for further details on this topic.

Valuation and pricing

Fund managers value their investment portfolio from time to time to ascertain the profit or losses since the last valuation. As a result of this, they are able to determine the amount that is attributable to each participant and the prices to be paid to the manager when issuing units to incoming holders. This also helps determine the prices to be paid by the manager when redeeming units for outgoing holders.

The Net Asset Value (NAV) of a fund is determined by valuation of the underlying securities and other assets and deducting liabilities and expenses. When valuing a fund, the following steps are taken:

- multiply the number of shares held in a security by its market price;
- aggregate the value(s) of each investment thus obtained;
- add uninvested cash to give the portfolio or capital value;
- add income received/receivable;
- deduct expenses, charges and taxes, including provisions, to give NAV.[30]

The buying and selling of shares are then determined by dividing NAV by the total number of shares or units in issue and, if applicable or permitted, adding or deducting the manager's charges.

30 Valuation method extracted from "Introduction to Fund Management" by Ray Russell, 2006.

Investor Relations

This chapter gives an overview of investor administration and performance management including benchmarking, yields and returns.

Investor Administration

Investor administration is about overseeing the issues that relate to investors such as registration, communication and dealing. Investment management firms outsource their investor administration to a third-party, i.e. custodian/depository.

Outsourcing

As funds get bigger, both in size and number of investors, outsourcing of processes such as registration becomes the most viable option. In order to ensure that the third party performs to the required service levels, a Service Level Agreement (SLA) that is clear and comprehensive is usually put in place and continually monitored as steadfastly as the firm's own operation.

It is worth noting that regulations delineate a basic division of duties and responsibilities between the investment manager and the trustee or the depository/custodian and recommend that these parties must be independent of each other. The rationale behind this is to offer basic investor protection by separating the principal function of making investment decisions from the physical custody and registered legal ownership of investments.

Dealing

Dealing in investment management is a process whereby the manager buys and sells shares or units. In open-ended funds the manager acts as a principal in the transaction, i.e. they buy and sell units on their own account and take decisions on cancellations and reissue of units that are redeemed.

As for close-ended funds, dealing is carried out on a stock exchange where the shares of the fund are listed and through a stockbroker. The dealing process for the shares of funds, like every other company, has to comply with the Financial Services Authority's Conduct of Business and/or Listing Rules.

All transactions have to be settled; therefore the settlement is effected by the manager on completion of the required details of the transaction and documentation. Settlement in this context means payment of monies to the trustee/OEIC for new units/shares and to holders of shares/units that are redeemed or bought back by the manager in accordance with relevant regulations and terms of business.

Certain rules apply to dealing and settlement for the manner in which receipts from investors are applied to the purchase of units/shares. Client Money Rules, for example, stipulate that monies received should be deposited in an escrow (specially designated) client account for 24 hours by the manager until purchase is made and settlement is due and applied to the purchase of units/shares thereafter.

Registration

An appointed registrar, transfer agent or the manager is usually responsible for the registration function. Registration entails keeping formal records of the legal ownership of shares and units issued by funds.

The following are some of the details that are recorded:

▓ name and address of the holder;
▓ number and type of shares/units held;
▓ date of registration of the holding.

Administrative activities carried out on these records by the registrar include:

▓ addition and deletion of holders;
▓ updating of personal details of holders;
▓ amendment of holdings as a result of issues and redemptions;
▓ changes to holdings on transfer;
▓ updates of the register to reflect conversions from one type of unit/share to another, splits or subdivision of high-value units;
▓ updates of the register to reflect switches between funds or sub-funds.

Integrity of the data is maintained in accordance with the Data Protection Act in the UK and similar acts in other countries.

Communication

Investment managers have to communicate material changes to the investors in the funds they are managing throughout the period that the investors are registered as holders in the funds. These changes are largely as a result of the introduction of new laws and regulations or amendment to existing ones, and have an impact on the important aspect of the fund's purpose or operation. This situation usually calls for a meeting of holders.

Reporting

Investment managers issue reports covering a fund's performance over a given period to investors and this period varies from fund to fund and from firm to firm. The report may contain:

▓ investment commentary;
▓ financial highlights including formal accounts and notes to the accounts;
▓ information about how the fund has been operated (comprehensive enough for investors to understand);
▓ the results of the manager's current investment decisions;
▓ the manager's future investment decisions and justification for them.

The table in Figure 6.1 shows an extract of financial highlights for a fictitious fund, Biz EuroGrowth Fund, for the period ended 28 June 2006 and the previous five fiscal years. This information is derived from the Fund's unaudited interim financial statements for the period ended 28 June 2006 and annual financial statements.

Figure 6.1 Biz EuroGrowth Fund for the period ended 28 June 2006

Investor Series	2006 (£bn)	2005 (£bn)	2004 (£bn)	2003 (£bn)	2002 (£bn)	2000 (£bn)
NET ASSET VALUE (NAV) PER UNIT						
Net Asset Value, Beginning of Period	8.07	7.94	7.82	7.56	9.94	10.84
Increase (Decrease) from Operations						
Total Revenue	0.15	0.18	0.27	0.72	(1.66)	(1.03)
Total Expenses	(0.06)	(0.12)	(0.12)	(0.11)	(0.13)	(0.15)
Realised Gains (Losses) for the period	(0.13)	(0.29)	(0.03)	(0.35)	(0.21)	0.02
Unrealised Gains(Losses) for the period	(0.13)	0.37	0.04	0.06	(0.39)	0.25
Total Increase (Decrease) from Operations	(0.17)	0.14	0.16	0.20	(2.39)	(0.91)
Distributions from:						
Income	0.00	0.00	0.00	0.00	0.00	0.00
Dividends	0.00	0.00	0.00	0.00	0.00	0.00
Capital Gains	0.00	0.00	0.00	0.00	0.00	0.00
Return of Capital	0.00	0.00	0.00	0.00	0.00	0.00
Total Distributions	0.00	0.00	0.00	0.00	0.00	0.00
Net Asset Value, End of Period	7.86	8.07	7.94	7.82	7.56	9.94

Distribution

Investment managers communicate the distribution of income from funds to investors along with cheques or advice and tax vouchers. The mode of communication and decisions on whether to distribute or reinvest income vary from one fund to another.

Changes

Changes to funds can be made or proposed for various reasons at the discretion of the manager. These changes have to be communicated to the investors and in some cases their approval has to be sought before the changes can be effected.

The changes in question include:

- investment objectives or policy;
- the name of the fund;
- the charging structure(which may require approval of both investors and regulators).

Charges

The procedures for communicating changes in the charging structure are dependent on whether the current level of charges is to be increased up to the maximum level stated in the fund documents, or if the maximum charge stated in the documents is to be exceeded. In the former case, the manager gives appropriate notice to investors when the charges are to be increased. In the latter case, however, the manager has to call a meeting with investors to present the proposal for approval.

Fund Mergers

When funds are merged, the investment manager usually calls for a meeting of investors in the decommissioned fund. Justifications for discontinuing the fund are set out in a set of proposals in a formal document accompanying a notice of meeting and provide investors with details of the continuing fund to enable them to make informed choices.

Conversion

Investors require notification of conversions of funds from one to type to another. For example, the conversion of unit trusts into OEICs requires special notification and approval from investors.

Meetings

As stated above, investment managers call for meetings with investors for various reasons. These meetings are conducted according to the normal conventions of meetings, but provisions are made for applicable regulations specific to the type of fund. For example, the FSA "old rules" require 10% of holders (investors) on record at a given date and eligible to attend meetings and cast votes.

Performance Management

Fund performance is a measure for the comparison of funds competing for investment. Fund performance is the acid test of fund management, and in the institutional context accurate measurement is a necessity. To this end, institutions measure the performance of each fund (and usually, for internal purposes, components of each fund) under their management. Performance is also measured by external firms that specialise in performance measurement. The leading performance measurement firms compile aggregate industry data showing how funds in general performed against given indices and peer groups over various time periods.

Performance management in investment management should not be confused with the IT discipline of performance management, which focuses on monitoring and managing the performance and availability of IT systems.

Sector Comparison

Sector comparison is an exercise that provides assistance to investors seeking to compare similar funds. In essence, investors get to compare life funds with other life funds and unit trusts with other unit trusts. Categorisation is not restricted to the broad classifications of life funds, pension funds and so on. There are subdivisions of these categories into managed funds compared with self-select

ISAs, endowment policies of differing investment horizons, i.e. a 10-year endowment policy compared with a 15-year policy.

As seen in Chapter 2, the trade body for retail funds (the IMA) defines performance categories for funds based on investment objectives and also on geographical emphasis and other criteria. The equivalent body for investment trusts, the Association of Investment Trusts (AITC) also has similar categories for investment trusts.

Some companies provide statistical analysis of individual fund performance over time. Notable among these companies is Standard and Poor's Micropal that provides data to investment managers and publishers for performance comparisons. The Standard & Poor's Micropal Star Ranking assists investors in evaluating the performance of a fund and the consistency of that performance relative to other funds in the sector. It is calculated using a fund's monthly performance relative to its sector average for each of the 36 months over the 3 years to date. The average and volatility of these 36 figures is used to calculate a fund's star rating.

S&P Fund Rating Process

A veritable fund rating process is the S&P Fund Rating Process and it is as described below.

Standard & Poor's ratings identify investment funds that have provided consistently strong performance year after year, relative to a meaningful peer group.

Comparison of apples to apples

The first step is to ensure that funds are being compared to an appropriate peer group. When shopping for a luxury car, the features and price of a Mercedes are not measured against those of a Volkswagen.

Instead, comparative information on other luxury cars – Audi or BMW – should be analysed. In the same way, it makes no sense to compare two very different types of investment fund.

Standard & Poor's recognises that fund categorisation is important for investors and investment professionals building asset allocation programmes. That's why it compares funds only to other funds that are similarly managed. S&P compares funds on the basis of their objectives using portfolio-level reviews to ensure homogeneity of universes.

Identification of consistent performers in each asset class

What's in a cumulative performance record? Looking at any list of top-performing funds, investors will likely find a few that have achieved their results on the strength of one spectacular year.

In some cases, top-ranked funds have turned in mediocre or even poor results in two out of three years. Investors and investment professionals who choose them are effectively betting that lightning will strike twice – and that managers will be able to duplicate their single exceptional year's return. Often, last year's star is this year's laggard.

And yet many investors will choose funds simply based on recent high returns. They may ignore other funds that have built long-term records by turning out consistently above-average performance within their investment category year after year after year. And because of the media's focus on each year's hot funds, many investors never hear about the funds that provide this kind of consistent performance.

Standard & Poor's identifies funds that deliver consistent performance by analysing absolute and risk-adjusted performance for each year over a three-year period. It gives each fund a quantitative score ranging from 1 to 100, comprising equal-weighted proportions of these two measures of historical return. Funds that score in the mid-second quartile or above are candidates for Standard & Poor's Fund Management Rating status.

Identification of disciplined, experienced management

The Standard & Poor's Fund Management Rating research process considers consistency of performance, but it recognises quantitative performance analysis is not enough. S&P believes that both quantitative performance data and qualitative fund management analysis are needed to provide a true measure of investment fund excellence.

Ratings

Funds that earn the Standard & Poor's Fund Management Rating are classified AAA to A. These funds, in Standard & Poor's view, demonstrate an ability to provide above-average consistent performance, along with the ability to adhere to a set investment process.

Management quality is a crucial element of consistent investment fund success. Standard & Poor's believes a strong management team, a clear investment philosophy and a well-defined investment process can have a significant impact on the consistency of a fund's performance. Evaluating managers requires a hands-on approach, including extensive face-to-face interviews, performed by experienced investment fund analysts.

S&P takes the view that it is only by understanding the minds behind the money that investors can increase their chances of selecting the most consistently performing funds. S&P believes that managers who have a clear philosophy and continually implement it through a disciplined process are more likely to be able to replicate their results.

Incorporate quantitative data with qualitative research

Thoroughly assessing management quality means examining issues such as the following.

Organisational strength

What is the organisation's history and structure? What other companies does it own and how might they affect the management of the fund? Does the organisation have a well-developed business strategy? Are there an overarching investment philosophy, an investment process and a strategy for managing risk?

87

Fund management team

What is the depth and stability of the fund management team? How many people support the fund manager and what is the reporting structure? What level of experience do team members have? How long have key people been managing the fund? How does the team generate and evaluate investment ideas? What research capabilities support the investment process?

Fund management/style consistency

What are the fund manager's experience, track record and philosophy? Has the manager run similar funds in the past at the same or different companies (especially if they have less than a three-year record at the current fund)? If so, what was the manager's previous track record? How well-defined is their investment process, including stock screening, portfolio construction and sector allocation? How does the philosophy of this fund fit with that of the fund management group? Has the manager stayed true to their stated style? How much risk has the manager taken to achieve the fund's returns? Is it consistent with the stated risk parameters? What resources are available, including people, systems and research? Does the fund manager have other responsibilities (i.e., managing other funds, serving on the fund sponsor's investment committee, marketing, etc.)?

Portfolio construction

What is the portfolio's benchmark? Are there constraints on sector weightings relative to the benchmark? What are the manager's guidelines on asset allocation and cash positions? How does the manager ensure that the portfolio remains consistent with their stated investment style? How does the manager feel about using derivatives or leverage? How concentrated do they prefer to keep the fund's portfolio? What are the manager's buy/sell disciplines? What are the portfolio manager's objectives for managing the portfolio's turnover and tax efficiency?

Performance

What major investment decisions were made over the past year and how have they worked out? What are the fund's current holdings and how have they changed recently? On what sectors and industries does the management team currently concentrate and how has that changed recently? What is the manager's explanation for periods of outperformance or underperformance?

There are no right or wrong answers to these questions. However, when a fund is managed with a consistent philosophy, style and portfolio construction over time, the belief is that it is more likely to provide above-average relative performance in the future.

Monitor funds on a continuous basis

Past performance by itself may not be a predictor of future results. And disciplined management and investment processes are important, but only if they can deliver consistent performance. Standard & Poor's Fund Management Rating research is unique in that it considers both kinds of information. It identifies the premier funds in each asset class – approximately 20% of funds in each universe – that have met the rigorous standards for both performance and management expertise. By emphasising the important link between management quality and consistency of performance, it can deliver more informed, stable conclusions than performance data alone allows.

It is important to concentrate on both consistent performance and management quality. While these factors don't change as rapidly as quarter-by-quarter performance results, investors and investment professionals must still be armed with timely, relevant updates and analyses to make informed decisions on a continuous basis.

Because of the focus on fundamentals, Standard & Poor's Fund Management Rating funds tend to merit their status longer than funds reflecting typical performance-based evaluations.

S&P monitors the funds that have achieved the Standard & Poor's Fund Management Rating status through a comprehensive process that tracks fund performance, management and portfolio holdings.

A new standard for investment fund research

S&P looks for long-term consistency in each of these areas as well as a demonstrated commitment to each fund's stated investment approach. The process is not mechanically driven by performance statistics.

Rather, it incorporates a more thorough understanding of manager philosophy, objectives and process. Because the company constantly monitors these factors, it is able to alert users to any significant changes in fund management, style or portfolio emphasis.

If Standard & Poor's changes its opinion on a fund, it is because Standard & Poor's has determined that there has been a fundamental change in the fund or its management, not simply a shift in short-term performance.

How to tell when a good fund turns bad

Almost all investors and investment professionals have had this experience: After conducting exhaustive research, investors/investment managers select a high-quality investment fund that meets a specific set of investment objectives, asset allocation needs and risk tolerance criteria. The fund's performance then declines. Is it a good fund that's experiencing temporary difficulties? Or have there been fundamental changes which indicate that the fund will no longer perform at its previous level of excellence?

A short period of underperformance doesn't always indicate that the investment manager has lost their touch. It may, in fact, simply demonstrate that the fund manager remains true to the fund's style regardless of short-term changes in market emphasis.

Standard & Poor's believes that several types of events – in conjunction with poor performance – may merit an in-depth review of a fund.

These events include:

- a change in fund management company ownership;
- a new portfolio manager;
- a significant shift in asset allocation;
- substantial drift in investment style.

Sustained underperformance

When the S&P monitoring process is alerted to these types of changes, it typically contacts management to gain a better understanding of what is happening.

Other companies such as Towers Perrin, a firm of actuaries, offer services to investors by way of periodic reviews of pension funds. Lipper, a Reuters company, provides investment managers with a windows-based fund performance desktop tool, Hindsight, for analysing US, European, Asian and offshore fund markets, which is designed for fund performance analysis.

Yields and Returns

The term "yield" is often used freely in our everyday lives to emphasise the viability of investment in some property hotspot in London or in Bansko in Bulgaria. Whilst this could be an amateur investor's perspective on yield, it is reasonably consistent with a more professional view of it.

An elementary definition of yield is as follows:

Yield is the annual rate of return for any investment and is expressed as a percentage.

This is a general definition of yield but readers will come across yield in other contexts such as in notes and bonds. There are variants of yield used in investment management such as income yield, historic distribution yield, current yield, forecast yield, portfolio yield and redemption yield.

The following are formulae used for calculating income yield, portfolio yield and redemption yield.

(1) Income Yield = $\dfrac{\text{Income for year}}{\text{Investment Cost}} \times 100\%$

(2) Portfolio Yield = $\dfrac{\text{Future annual income of current portfolio}}{\text{Cost of buying portfolio}} \times 100\%$

The above formulae are relevant to equity-based funds or funds that are not influenced by fixed dated stocks but for such stocks[31] and for funds that contain such stocks, the formula for redemption yield is more relevant.

31 Securities that have a specified remaining life or duration to maturity.

(3) Redemption Yield = $\sqrt[n]{\dfrac{\text{Interest income for the period}[32] + \text{Maturity proceeds}[33]}{\text{Initial cost/Current value of investment}}} - 1 \times 100\%$

where n = the number of years to maturity.

Benchmarking

In order to grasp the concept of benchmarks, the terms "absolute performance" and "relative performance" will be defined. Absolute performance can be defined as the performance of a fund over a period of time while relative performance is more the performance of a fund assessed against a benchmark.

In the UK and the USA, two of the world's most sophisticated fund management markets, the tradition is for institutions to manage client money relative to benchmarks. For example, an institution can be proud of its achievements if it has generated a return of 8% when the average manager generates a 6% return.

As stated in Chapter 2, an index measures changes over time. While an index can assist an investment manager with the timing of investment decisions, by observed trends of prices as measured by the index and in the measuring of an individual fund's performance relative to the index, it can also provide a mechanism for constructing a benchmark portfolio according to a selected asset allocation.

The following is an example of how a benchmark return can be calculated using movements over a given year of a number of indices relevant to geographical locations in which a fund's assets are allocated.

The trustees of a £100m BigBiz Pension Fund specified at the beginning of 2007 a geographic asset allocation as follows:

- UK: 60%
- Japan: 20%
- USA: 20%

The relevant indices for these geographical locations, FTSE, S&P and Nikkei, had movements of +20%, +30% and -20% respectively over the course of the year.

The total return for the year of the fund manager, Billy Bob, was calculated to be 25% and during the year there was no inflow of cash into the fund.

The calculation of the growth of the benchmark portfolio based on the asset allocation and the rise and fall of the indices is as follows:

{(100 x 0.6) x 1.2} + {(100 x 0.2) x 1.3} + {(100 x 0.2) x 0.80} = £114m

The benchmark portfolio has grown from £100m to £114m and since Billy Bob's return was 25%, his portfolio has grown to £125m and he has outperformed

32 Accrued interest on a security over the remaining years to maturity.
33 Amount paid to holders on maturity of the security, e.g. nominal value of a bond.

the benchmark set by reference to selected indices which emulate the specified geographical distribution of the portfolio. On the strength of his performance, the trustees have a "star" fund manager in Billy Bob.

Volatility

The performance movement of a fund over a certain period is called its volatility. Funds whose performance moves sharply are said to have high volatility. Those with stable performances have low volatility. Checking fund volatility is an important factor in an investment decision.

Volatility is measured by the standard deviation of the change in value of a financial instrument with a specific time horizon. It is often used to quantify the risk of the instrument over that time period. Volatility is typically expressed in annualised terms, and it may be either an absolute number (£5) or a fraction of the initial value (5%).

The most common measure of volatility is historical volatility (or ex-post volatility) which is the volatility of a financial instrument based on historical returns. This phrase is used particularly when distinguishing between the actual volatility of an instrument in the past, and the current (ex-ante, or forward-looking) volatility implied by the market.

Risk-adjusted Performance Management

Having discussed the concept of volatility, it can be seen that performance measurement is not reduced to the evaluation of fund returns alone, but also integrates other fund elements that investors factor into their investment decisions, such as the measure of risk taken.

Modern portfolio theory established the quantitative link that exists between portfolio risk and return. The Capital Asset Pricing Model (CAPM) developed by William Sharpe in 1964 highlighted the notion of rewarding risk and produced the first performance indicators: risk-adjusted ratios (Sharpe ratio, information ratio) and differential returns compared to benchmarks (alphas).[34] The Sharpe ratio is the simplest and best known performance measure.

The definition of the Sharpe Ratio is:

$$S(x) = (r_x - R_f) / StdDev(x)\ [35]$$

Where:
x is some investment
r_x is the average annual rate of return of x
R_f is the best available rate of return of a "risk-free" security (i.e. cash)
StdDev(x) is the standard deviation of r_x

The CAPM formula takes into account an asset's (in a fund) sensitivity to non-diversifiable risk (also known as systematic risk or market risk), in a number

34 Alpha – A measure of performance on a risk-adjusted basis.
35 Source: www.moneychimp.com/articles/risk/sharpe_ratio.htm.

often referred to as beta[36] (ß) in the financial industry, as well as the expected return of the market and the expected return of a theoretical risk-free asset.

The CAPM formula is:

ra = rf + [ß x (rm – rf)]

Where:

ra = expected return on the security

rf = risk-free rate for the expected holding period of the asset

ß = the security's beta

rm = return on a diversified market portfolio

rm – rf = the difference between the market portfolio return and the risk-free rate, i.e. the market risk premium.

The formulae displayed in this chapter are meant to show readers the formulae that investment managers use in the course of their investment business and, as such, there will not be any further analysis for the sake of simplicity.

36 Beta – A measure of the volatility, or systematic risk, of a security or a portfolio in comparison to the market as a whole.

Derivatives Operations in the Investment Management Industry

This chapter describes the derivative operations in the investment management industry and also the function of custodians in OTC derivatives trading.

Derivative Operations[37]

The area of Derivative Operations is enormously important and challenging to Investment Management firms. The recent boom in derivative use on the buy-side, particularly in the area of over-the-counter (OTC) contracts, has fundamentally altered the way that money is managed – leading to new products, investment processes and a whole raft of operational requirements which are either completely new to investment managers, or fundamentally altered by the advent of these new asset types.

Operational models for derivative processing are still emerging in the buy-side and so there is a temptation to 'borrow' technology and process approaches from Investment Banking firms, who have traded derivatives at high volume for a significantly longer period of time. At a high-level, this approach appears to work because the Bank and Manager are effectively participating in two sides of the same trade – as shown in the Credit Default Swap (CDS) trade example below.

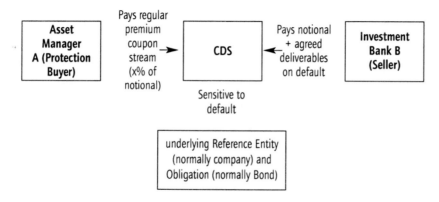

TRADE DETAILS

Trade Date	02 January 2007
Effective Date	03 January 2007
Scheduled Termination	03 January 2012
Floating Rate Payer ("Seller")	Investment Bank A
Fixed Rate Payer ("Buyer")	Asset Manager B
Calculation Agent	Seller
Calculation Agent City	London
Business Day	London
Business Day Convention	Modified Following
Reference Entity	Company C Ltd
Reference Obligation Primary Obligor	Company C

37   Contributed by Troy Travlos of Investment Horizon.

Maturity	20 May 2019
Coupon	6%
Identifier	XXX
Original Issue Amount	GBP 50,000,000
Reference Price	100%
All Guarantees	Not Applicable

FIXED PAYMENTS

Fixed Rate Payer	Buyer
Calculation Amount	GBP 10,000,000
Fixed Rate	0.41% p.a.
Fixed Rate Payer Payment	3 Apr, 3 Jul, 3 Oct, 3 Jan repeats quarterly
Fixed Rate Day Count	Actual / 365

FLOATING PAYMENTS

Floating Rate Payer	Seller
Calculation Amount	GBP 10,000,000
Conditions to Payment	Credit Event Notice (Notifying Parties: Buyer or Seller)
Notice of Publicly Available Information: Applicable (Public Source: Standard Public Sources. Specified Number: Two)	
Credit Events Bankruptcy	Bankruptcy
Failure to Pay	(Grace Period Extension: Not Applicable. Payment Requirement: GBP 1,000,000)

SETTLEMENT TERMS

(There is a range of standard settlement options defined by ISDA, too numerous to detail in this chapter but available for a range of instrument types at www.isda.org)

However, the regulatory and business realities of Investment Management, particularly the trend to process all asset types within a single Operations area, are fundamentally different to the product-segregated approach prevalent in Investment Banking. To outline the operational impacts of derivative use on the buy-side, it is useful to consider the operational life-cycle steps of the trade in question.

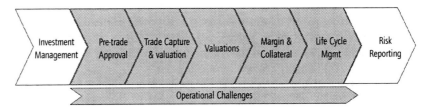

Pre-trade approval

Investment Managers have a range of compliance regimes under which they manage money. These depend on the type of client, and might be regulatory, such as the FSA COLL regulations covering collective investment schemes within the UK, or might be specified by the individual client, as in segregated institutional pension mandates.

Part of the objective of investing in derivatives, especially OTCs, is to access the investment precision that they provide. Derivatives are traded for this isolated risk and return exposure to almost any market variable, and can also result in leverage – where the initial value of the derivative may be zero, or very low, but market movements can result in large gains or losses. For this reason, regulators and clients are expanding the rules governing Investment Management to include more rigorous and appropriate controls.

The traditional model for pre-trade approval normally centres on a compliance platform, pre-loaded with instrument and portfolio data, which validates proposed trades to ensure that the resulting portfolio will still be compliant with a set of pre-configured rules. These specific tests might include:

- Identification of whether an asset is allowed to be traded, based on a range of properties including type (e.g. option), issuer (e.g. Ford) or credit rating (e.g. only trade A- or greater);
- Concentration limits, for example no more than 10% exposure to a single company;
- Portfolio impacts (e.g. portfolio duration must remain below 7.5 years post-trade).

All of these traditional rules apply to derivatives – and the model is fairly straightforward for exchange-traded futures and options, where the instruments are defined and understood before trading, and so can be included in the compliance universe with more traditional equities and bonds. However, the model becomes more complex for OTCs, where the underlying *instrument* is effectively bespoke, and so only defined at the point of trade.

Given this context, key operational considerations around pre-trade approval for derivatives include:

- **Basic counterparty checks** – validating that ISDA (International Swaps and Derivatives Association) agreements, which cover bilateral engagement between derivative trading parties, are present for the counterparty proposed, and that trading with the counterparty is within any set limits. This is similar to traditional "allowed broker" checks.
- **Calculating instrument exposure** – in many cases, compliance checks for derivative trades will not be linked to the value of the trade, but to the underlying exposure it provides. For OTC derivatives, these measures, which could include duration, credit duration, delta-adjusted exposure or others, will need to be calculated *internally* at the point of trade proposal. This is a fundamental difference from the cash/physical asset model, where expo-

sure analytics can normally be downloaded from data vendors along with price information.

- **Bridging derivative gaps in the compliance platform** – because exposure metrics for derivative compliance checking are internally calculated, there is the need to feed these calculations into the relevant compliance engine. This can be carried our by direct integration with the analytic engine, or by pre-populating the proposed instrument details (along with estimated exposures) as a precursor to the actual compliance check.
- **Calculating portfolio exposure** – for some emerging mandate limits, e.g. Value at Risk (VaR), impacts need to be calculated in the context of the existing portfolio because the component VaR of the trade is not simply added to the portfolio's existing exposure. This requirement for portfolio-level recalculation is more normally covered by specialist Risk Systems, and is appropriate for pre-trade approval if the trade is significant to the risk budget of the fund.
- **Checks linked to collateral processing** – funds with significant derivative use are likely to have large collateralised positions. For pre-trade approval purposes, it is important to understand and measure uncollateralised (net) credit exposure, and also to flag any positions pledged as collateral, to avoid inadvertent sale.

Transaction capture

Transaction capture is probably the most important stage of a derivative life cycle. Completeness of transaction capture (again, particularly for OTC derivatives) is absolutely key to improving automation and scalability, and to reducing downstream errors.

The paradigm shift for OTC derivatives is that transaction capture normally involves the construction of an entirely new instrument. A typical equity or bond trade will effectively raise an order to buy or sell units in a particular asset, which is likely to already exist on the Investment Manager's trading platform, and this leads to a segregation of roles:

- The Data Operations function in the Back Office is responsible for initial set-up of the tradable instrument universe; it is typically performed at a bulk index or market level, with ad hoc additions of new issues to keep the investable universe, which is finite, broadly complete.
- During the investment process, Investment Managers in the Front Office will raise orders on the instruments – specifying transaction quantity, price, commission and broker details – but will only need to identify the instrument in question.

With OTC derivatives, this distinction becomes blurred – Fund Managers and Dealers are responsible for creating the specific trade from an infinite universe of potential OTC trades that might be executed, and this drives on-the-fly construction of instrument data to support the trading, accounting and life-cycle processing of the trade in downstream platforms.

Important considerations to take into account when designing or enhancing systems and processes to deal with OTCs include:

- **Capturing the whole trade** – ensuring that the concept of "trade capture" includes instrument terms and conditions as well as the transaction details. These should be gathered at a sufficient level of detail to support set-up of the OTCs in downstream platforms. For the CDS example above, this would include underlying reference obligation and entity, maturity, coupon rates and frequencies, event conditions, reset frequencies and patterns, stub dates, etc.
- **Dealing with new derivative "shapes"** – as new and more complex derivatives emerge frequently, the trade capture platform should be able to support extended capture of new "flavours" of derivative instrument through configuration, rather than requiring major system upgrades.
- **Integrating decision support analytics** – in order to support the dealing process, some analytic capability is often useful to provide theoretical pricing for comparison, or to back out relevant execution terms of the instrument such as the "fair market" fixed rate for fixed/floating swaps, which will result in a par- (or zero-)value trade.
- **Templating repeatable information** – market-convention information for OTCs, such as accrual and roll conventions, coupon reset patterns etc., are often assumed to be "standard" terms by fund mangers, but still form part of the agreement with the counterparty and need to be captured and agreed as part of the trade. Systems implemented for trade capture should template this information, where possible, to prevent keying omissions and errors.
- **Enforcing appropriate automation** – although OTCs are theoretically completely flexible, market standards are emerging to automate the confirmation (and other related functions) of some regularly traded OTC derivatives, particularly simple Interest Rate and Credit Default Swaps, and some Options. For these instruments, the trade capture platform should capture sufficient detail (based on templated information) to support automated connectivity to confirmation platforms such as SwapsWire and DTCC. Conformance with these services implies significant constraints on the flexibility of trading, and the trade capture platform should be able to enforce this for "automatable" asset classes. However, the platform will still need to support exotic and structured trades – with more variable terms and conditions, normally contained in extended term sheets – and so must be able to apply different levels of trade constraint, appropriate to the automation level of the asset type in question.

Pricing

Pricing of derivatives raises another important capability requirement for investment managers. For cash/physical instruments, and also exchange-traded derivatives, market prices are typically available (liquidity allowing) from external data providers, who consolidate and validate prices from a range of sources.

Price feeds may also include analytic information – durations, yields, greeks (option sensitivities) and other exposure measures. However, with OTC derivatives, the pricing of derivatives become more complex, as the price of any one contract is specific to the terms of that contract, and is not generally common across the markets.

The capability for derivative pricing can be performed at a simple level (sourcing prices from counterparties) or at a more complex level (by deriving theoretical pricing in an internal application, or through use of an external pricing service). There are, however, a range of considerations that should be taken into account when implementing this capability:

- **Requirements for internal modelling** – internal platforms are often capable of a range of calculation and analytic functions. These systems can be utilised to provide theoretical pricing for OTC derivative positions, but this will depend on a supply of clean, validated market data to support price calculations, and may have shortcomings in catering for certain asset classes. The market data update cycle should be synchronised with the physical asset price update point, to maximise cross-asset price concordance.
- **Availability of external valuation providers** – evaluated prices are available from trade counterparties, but there are often issues with frequency, and independence of valuation. Emerging European legislation is also beginning to require external, independent price validation for OTCs in certain products, and an automation mechanism is required to exchange terms and conditions and price data with the valuation provider.
- **Internal consolidation and reconciliation** – the complexity of OTC pricing in cross-asset Investment Management firms means that a single provider is often not feasible for all derivative types. Multi-source pricing implies a requirement for centralised price sourcing, validation and reconciliation across systems (and trade counterparties).

Margin and collateral payments

Margin and collateral management for derivatives assume great importance as these instruments are used more extensively within portfolios. Funds with significant derivative exposure will result in large collateral pools and movements, and the disposition of this collateral pool will significantly impact portfolio risk and performance.

Margin movements for exchange-traded instruments are well understood in the industry, and follow a consistent model, but OTC instruments normally require a different approach to collateral management, including some or all of the following considerations:

- **The base collateral agreement** – normally designed as a bilateral agreement, where a party's net derivative position (the aggregate NPV, or Net Present Value, of all derivative positions under a particular ISDA) is used to drive a call or recall of collateral. If one party has a long derivative position (including the effects of any collateral currently in place), they will make a call on their counterparty, who will provide a cash collateral deposit (or equivalent non-cash collateral, with an appropriate margin). This collateral movement is designed to cover the first party's effective credit exposure by providing assets equivalent to the outstanding value of all derivative trades under the agreement, effectively neutralising almost all credit risk between counterparties.

- **Regular valuation of collateralised positions** – collateral calls can occur on any basis agreed by the parties, but are more generally moving towards daily movements within the industry. This implies a requirement for Investment Managers to value their derivative positions on an equivalent (daily) basis.
- **Eligible collateral** – collateral calls can be provided by cash (normally of equivalent value) or by eligible non-cash collateral, which will be specified in the supporting documentation of the applicable ISDA agreement governing the trade. A non-cash collateral band might refer to "A- GBP Bonds: margin 15%", meaning that £1.15M notional value of bonds would be required to cover a collateral call of £1M.
- **Processes for collateral call, recall and dispute** – the rules for collateral movement can vary between counterparties, but normally include a process for valuing the collateralised position, accounting for the impact of current collateral, making a call, agreeing or disputing that call, and then making an eligible collateral transfer based on collateral margins, minimum transfer amounts and rounding rules. These workflow rules are typically embedded within collateral management platforms or services.
- **Income synthesis** – where a bond or equity has an income event while placed as collateral (e.g. a coupon payment), this income is normally passed on to the provider of the collateral. This function is again normally supported by specialist collateral systems or service providers.
- **Rehypothecation** – greater use of derivatives can result in large pools of collateral. If a party is in receipt of large non-cash collateral placements from their counterparty, they are often entitled to rehypothecate those assets (e.g. for loan or repo) to generate additional income. The decision on how to improve the performance impact of collateral is, in reality, an investment decision, but tools and processes to support this should be considered as part of any derivatives scale-up.

Event and life-cycle management

Derivative contracts – particularly OTCs – often result in a set of life-cycle events which require specific workflow control and processing. Certain accounting systems are being improved to support derivative event management, but many incumbent platforms, designed specifically to service bonds and equities, and extended to support derivative value-based accounting, have shortcomings in this area – resulting in manual workarounds to process life-cycle events, which are likely to include:

101

- Reset agreements
- Coupon payments
- Novations
- Partial unwinds
- Credit events
- Exercise
- Expiry
- Knock-ins/knock-outs

Each of these events is likely to result in a processing impact to the downstream accounting platform, and may have a range of controlled processes to follow. Consideration of the following features is important:

- **Event calendar generation** – most derivative events will happen in accordance with a pre-agreed schedule or in response to a market event (e.g. default) or investment decision (e.g. early exercise). These events may require some controlled processing, but will generally result in a future cash flow or underlying security transfer. The key operational challenge in this area is to centrally identify and control these events.
- **Integration with downstream platforms** – the event calendar may be the master source for precise derivative cash flow information, and may need to feed data into downstream platforms (e.g. performance attribution systems) to supplement data which is available at a less granular level in the fund accounting platform.

Specific platforms and external services are now available in the market, which cater for the control and management of derivative life-cycle events.

Specific operational challenges

In summary, the advent of derivatives in Investment Management (and OTC derivatives in particular) presents a range of operational challenges for firms looking to scale up their use of these instruments. The impacts of these changes cover all platforms from trade capture to reporting, but there are certain key areas which involve new or complex capability, and should receive special consideration when looking to address these challenges:

- **Trade Capture** – begin with the end in mind. OTC trades contain more information than cash physical transactions. A key derivative-linked challenge is to be able to capture terms and conditions data at the point of trade, and the trade capture system must be flexible enough to capture complex instruments, and to rapidly incorporate new instrument structures as they emerge.
- **Event Management** – looking after the post-trade lifecycle. Complex derivative instruments all generally produce the same life-cycle results – cash flows, resets and deliveries of underlying securities. Holistic management of these events in a single platform allows for automation and improved control over an entire range of derivative types.

▓ **Valuation** – providing access to a range of valuation services. Valuation of derivative instruments is a complex function, and for OTCs has to be carried out by one or both parties to each trade (or outsourced to an independent provider). A range of valuation sources, both internal and external, are likely to be required – driving up operational requirements around data sourcing, complex service connectivity and multi-source price reconciliation.

▓ **Collateral management** – anticipating additional capability. Collateral management covers a greater and greater scope of "assets under management", as funds take on large long or short derivative positions. Extensive use of derivatives across fund ranges, and dealing with numerous counterparties, leads to a requirement for automation and efficiency in this process, which often implies new system or service capability.

Functions of Custodians in OTC Derivatives Trade

The concept of custody was discussed earlier in Chapter 1 and how it relates to investment management. In this section the functions of Custodians in the OTC derivatives trading process will be discussed.

The role of the custodian in the OTC derivatives marketplace is to offer various services to investment managers to ensure that their OTC contracts are settled in time. The various functions custodians perform include Contract Maintenance, Event Processing, Valuation and Payment Calculation, Payment and Settlement, Reconciliation, Collateral Management, Account Maintenance and Reporting.

Contract Maintenance

The main role of custodians in contract maintenance is to ensure that details of the contracts are maintained throughout the various stages of the contract and these include:

▓ Maintenance of the trade details and confirmations sent by the client with respect to:
  ▓ New Trades
  ▓ Trade Modification, i.e. amendment of trade details such as the notional, etc.
  ▓ Assignment
  ▓ Exercise/ Termination (partial or full).
▓ Requisition of transaction details from the client/counterparty by making use of:
  ▓ Manual delivery or data feed in Financial Products Mark-Up Language (FpML)
  ▓ Confirmations either in paper form (that can be manually updated) or sourced from companies such as DTCC.

103

■ Contract shredding: this involves cancelling offsetting contracts using services from companies such as TriOptima.[38]

Event Processing

A number of the various events that occur during the life cycle of a contract are managed by custodians. These events include the following:

■ receipt of credit event notices;
■ processing of corporate action events;
■ processing of early termination and assignment events;
■ processing of requests like portfolio rebalancing, and cancellations or annulments;
■ triggering collection of contingent payment from the counterparty;
■ periodic rate resets for Interest Rate Swaps (IRS);
■ triggering appropriate action contained in the contract on default of a counterparty (for instruments such as IRS).

Valuation and Payment Calculation

The valuation of positions and collateral, and the computation of payment requirements throughout the lifecycle of the contract are the responsibility of the custodian. The various functions include the following:

■ valuation of positions and collateral offered against each position for exposure monitoring
■ marking-to-market individual positions and collateral securities regularly, with previously agreed valuation model and parameters and also market data feeds;
■ calculation of payments due on periodic intervals and quarterly rolls;
■ bilateral netting of payments to be effected;
■ payment matching with service providers such as DTCC's Deriv/Serv;
■ sending these inputs to collateral manager group.

Payment and Settlement

Custodians handle the processing of payment and settlement instructions received from the client. The main functions amongst others are:

■ Carrying out payment instructions in respect of:
    ■ periodic cash flows and exchange of principal;
    ■ collection of the contingent payment on the occurrence of a credit event;
    ■ close-out netting in case of default by a counterparty, premature termination of contract, and so on;

38 TriOptima is an international financial technology company that is solving some of the most challenging post-trade processing problems in the OTC derivatives market.

- acceptance of delivery of collateral amount or posting collateral amount on behalf of the client.
- Interaction with operations/back office in the investment management (client) companies.

Reconciliation

Reconciliation of cash/collateral movements throughout the life cycle of the contract is carried out by custodians. The main roles include:

- monitoring and reconciling;
- collateral receipt/substitution;
- collateral release;
- periodic cash flow booking.

Collateral management

Collateral management is another important service offered by custodians. The service offerings throughout the life cycle of the contract include:

- evaluation of the terms of ISDA Credit Support Annex;
- checking availability of initial/suitable collateral cover at the start/during the life of the contract;
- exposure monitoring – movement of value of collateral against position(s) held:
    - act upon instances of under-collateralisation or over-collateralisation as per contract/master agreement between counterparties;
    - process substitution of collateral securities by different (eligible) securities;
    - place margin call in case of under-collateralisation;
    - release collateral in the instances of over-collateralisation;
    - monitor receipt/delivery of collateral.
- triggering default in the instance of breach of collateral conditions;
- coordinating with credit/risk management teams in direct organisations.

Account Maintenance

Account maintenance includes "housekeeping" activities involving the maintenance of the client account, starting from the negotiation through collateral management until the settlement of the trade. These activities include the following:

- Maintenance of the details of the ISDA master agreement and specific master agreements, if any;
- Execution of bilateral/tripartite agreements with clients concerning the operation of accounts;
- Communication with clients regarding rights and responsibilities of client and custodian under different circumstances;

■ Maintenance of cash and collateral accounts including assignment of collateral to different trade types;

■ Carrying out instructions received in the course of event processing;

■ Client reporting.

Miscellaneous Reporting Activities

Other service offerings from custodians include:

■ Policy and process documentation;

■ Regulatory reporting.

Innovations in the industry

There are innovations proposed by players in this segment to speed up trade capture and post-trade settlement processes by eliminating the existing bottlenecks. An example of the initiatives taken up includes Omgeo[39] Connect linking with DTCC Deriv/Serv to automate processing of OTC Derivatives trades. In linking the two services, Omgeo Connect clients will be able to access Omgeo Central TradeManager[SM] (Omgeo CTM), Omgeo OASYS-TradeMatch[SM] and DTCC Deriv/Serv via a single hub. Omgeo Connect will extend its XML specification to capture the data relevant to OTC derivatives, transform this data into industry-standard FpML messages, and route these messages to DTCC Deriv/ Serv via an MQ interface. Post matching, Omgeo Connect will receive status messages from DTCC/SERV, transform these messages, and pass them back to the investment manager via their Omgeo Connect interface.[40]

39 Omgeo develop and deploy post-trade, pre-settlement solutions..
40 Source: www.isda.org/c_and_a/pdf/ISDA-Operations-Survey-2006.pdf.

Systems used in Investment Management

8

This chapter describes some of the common systems used in the investment management industry and the key trends that affect investment managers and providers.

Introduction

The investment management industry is changing rapidly, not only in the way business is conducted but also in the attitude towards compliance and governance. Investment customers are more demanding in that they expect better returns on their investments and the regulatory climate is also more restrictive with new regulations such as MiFID putting the industry under far greater scrutiny than at any point in the past.

Against this backdrop, investment management firms have to react to these changes and deploy best-of-breed systems for processes such as trading, portfolio management and performance management. It is increasingly important in recent times for investment managers to select the best trading systems as buy-side trading is increasingly becoming an integral part of the investment process.

According to Celent, total global spending by asset managers on trading systems will grow from US$634 million in 2006 to US$757 million by 2010, an average annual growth rate of 4.6%.

Global Asset Management Asset Spend

Source: Celent Consulting

Notable Systems Used In Investment Management

The market for investment management software is dominated by Charles River Development and LatentZero. IT professionals working in investment management will come across the systems from these vendors as most companies in this sector use either of these vendor's products for trading, order management compliance and portfolio management.

A description of systems and their benefits are presented in this section as contributed by the individual systems' vendors. The following vendors contributed detailed information about their systems:

■ Charles River
■ LatentZero
■ Statspro
■ Linedata
■ DST International

Vendor: LatentZero
System: Capstone
Overview

Capstone enables asset managers on the buy-side to deliver maximum performance and keep up to date with a constantly changing market. It handles increased volume trades in real time without loss of performance and manages compliance with an increasing number of regulations and complex client mandates, while its multi-asset-class capabilities enable asset managers to diversify portfolios for maximum returns. The Service-Oriented, Event-Driven technical architecture (SOA/EDA) which underpins Capstone is state of the art and works seamlessly with any other front-, middle- or back-office technology. It provides a 24x7 high-performance solution that is scalable, and can be implemented globally from a single installation. Capstone can be deployed as a complete solution of compliance, portfolio analysis, and order and execution management, or can have each of these elements installed separately and integrated with legacy and back-office systems – giving users choice and complete control over their trading environment.

Capstone is an asset management engine that dynamically models, allocates and monitors accounts before, during and after the trading day in true real time. It delivers maximum performance combined with fail-safe client mandates and regulatory compliance across all asset classes. Capstone is used by nine of the world's top ten asset managers, and handles more than $8 trillion assets under management.

Capstone can be deployed as a stand-alone platform to create a state-of-the-art trading desk. Alternatively, its constituent elements can be installed as individual components and seamlessly integrated with existing back-office and legacy systems.

The three main components of Capstone are: Tesseract, a portfolio analysis and modelling application; Minerva for order management and trading; and Sentinel for pre- and post-trade compliance management.

Capstone is underpinned by its multi-tiered, message-based, event-driven architecture that is designed to support the specific needs of the asset management industry. It achieves throughput levels greatly in excess of those achieved by systems using standard databases, while its open design offers an extremely high degree of scalability and flexibility. This enables LatentZero technology to be deployed globally from a single implementation – creating a single, consolidated buy-side system at a fraction of the time and cost of a multi-site roll-out.

The three core elements within Capstone break down as follows.

109

Capstone Tesseract

Tesseract is a decision support and portfolio management system. It is adaptable and customisable, giving asset managers the freedom to view portfolios to match the way they work. Because Tesseract is integrated into the workflow, it provides them with a single place to see all exposures and opportunities.

Key features are:

- The facility to dissect portfolios, analyse the risk profile of each holding, calculate order requirements for precise balancing, and create reports, including real-time P&L and heat-mapped deltas.
- Integration with other key systems on the desk to enable asset managers to make informed decisions across all asset classes.
- Intuitive graphical user interface that ensures unrivalled ease of use.
- Rigorous, real-time portfolio analysis using live market-data sources.

Capstone Sentinel™

Sentinel is the industry-leading compliance solution and is used by nine of the world's top ten asset management companies. It has a comprehensive rule library that is updated as and when new regulations come in to force.

Key features are:

- Reliability, flexibility, adaptability and scalability, offering true real-time compliance across all asset classes throughout the entire workflow of a trade.
- Rule-based technology that can easily be applied to even the most complex client mandates. Sentinel is aimed at business users who understand trading restrictions, rather than IT managers. Its intuitive rule builder enables non-technical users to construct a compliance rule and put it into production in minutes.
- Comprehensive audit trail, incorporating real-time and historical data; and contains input points that enable different users to check incidents and approve changes.
- Integration with other components in the Capstone suite or deployed as a stand-alone offering. It is also easily integrated with clients' legacy systems.
- User-definable workflows that ensure compliance, regardless of the way an asset manager chooses to work. Detected incidents can also be managed before they become an official breach.
- User-definable web-based and Crystal reports draw on real-time market information to provide comprehensive status updates, and details of all actions taken from detection to resolution.

Capstone Minerva

Minerva is a 24x7 global order management and trading system. It is designed to support the specific needs of the asset management industry and can be deployed globally from a single installation.

Key features are:

- Throughput levels greatly in excess of systems using standard databases. Its open architecture offers an extremely high level of scalability and flexibility, and also integrates easily with legacy systems.
- Truly global, real-time, multi-location platform, with highly configurable workflows and trade screens designed to fully support trading of all instruments. It enables traders to manage order flows from different managers on one blotter, provides access to the industry-leading data providers through pre-built feeds, filters information, and presents users with a consolidated view of their current positions, relationships and activity.
- True multi-asset-class capability, including equities, fixed income, foreign exchange and derivatives.
- Open architecture that enables it to work seamlessly with any front- or back-office systems, and is adaptable to meet clients' rapidly changing order and execution management requirements.
- Fully automated trading capabilities, including Direct Market Access (DMA), algorithmic trading, and pre-trade analytics. Full FIX[41] support for easy access to brokers, exchanges, Electronic Communication Networks (ECNs) and alternative trading venues to ensure best execution.
- Full integration with complete execution management system, offering full audit trail, better workflow control, increased pools of liquidity and more agile upgrades in a single application.

Vendor: Charles River Development
System: Charles River Investment Management System
Overview of Charles River and its System

Charles River provides software and services to over 235[42] investment managers in the global mutual fund, banking, pension, hedge fund, wealth management and insurance industries. It provides asset managers with complete trade-cycle support from portfolio management, trading and compliance to post-trade processing.

The Charles River Investment Management System (Charles River IMS)

The Charles River Investment Management System (Charles River IMS) aims to improve performance and streamline trade execution and processing. Portfolio managers, dealers and traders, and operations and compliance officers use this software suite for all security types to streamline, automate and enhance investment management operations.

---

41 Financial eXchange Protocol (see www.fixprotocol.org/) is a standard technology language used in the financial services industry. It is a series of messaging specifications for the electronic communication of trade-related messages. It was developed through the collaboration of banks, broker-dealers, exchanges, industry utilities and associations, institutional investors and information technology providers from around the world.

42 Figure in December 2006.

The components of the system are:

- **Charles River Manager** – facilitates global portfolio management and strategy analysis;
- **Charles River Trader** – designed for trading and order management, this module includes real-time electronic, FIX trading via the Charles River Network;[43]
- **Charles River Compliance** – enables the real-time monitoring of compliance rules to ensure trading activity is aligned with regulatory, company-related, fund and client mandates;
- **Charles River Post-Trade** – centralises trade matching, confirmation and settlement process, completing the trade cycle.

Technology and Architecture

The quality of systems in the financial industry can be assessed effectively in terms of the technology they employ. In order to respond quickly to rapidly changing, dynamic market conditions, the technology used by asset managers needs to have a robust architecture that is scalable (i.e. can handle business growth), flexible, open and designed to perform efficiently.

Since Charles River IMS is built on industry-standard technology (such as Java, Microsoft.NET, C# and Web services), the products are easy to implement and integrate with other systems. This addresses a key challenge commonly faced in the financial services industry. Businesses implement different systems to address varying processes over a period of time and require all new systems to integrate with the existing environment.

Who uses Charles River IMS?

All of Charles River's clients have one thing in common: they maximise their clients' assets by investing them in the financial markets.

Since Charles River IMS addresses the trade life cycle from front to middle office, there are many users of the system within asset management firms and departments. In the front office, trading and portfolio management teams take strategic trading decisions and execute these using Charles River Manager and Charles River Trader. Compliance officers can manage and respond to compliance issues and data, view the underlying data and use Charles River Compliance as a central source for all compliance rules. Operations and trade settlement teams can also use the post-trade module to match accounting details and ensure trades are reconciled and put through to the custodian for settlement.

---

43 The Charles River Network is a fully managed private financial network providing Charles River IMS clients with real-time FIX-based electronic connectivity to the global institutional investment community. It is built on the BT Radianz global network.

What are its unique features?

The key features that make Charles River IMS unique are its technology architecture, execution management capabilities, broad financial instrument coverage and deep compliance rule-making abilities. It offers the breadth and depth of features and functionality required to address all the idiosyncratic needs of asset managers in different markets around the globe.

System: Statpro
Vendor: Statpro
Overview

StatPro is a global provider of portfolio analytics and market data for the asset management industry. The company offers data and tools for risk management, fixed income attribution analysis, performance measurement and attribution analysis, Global Investment Performance Standard (GIPS), compliance, and enterprise-wide compliance and reporting.

- **StatPro Data Services** offers valuation data and analytical measures covering worldwide equities, bonds, indices and other assets.
- **StatPro Risk Management** combines the most comprehensive risk analysis with a centralised daily risk-profile data service to provide an unequalled capacity to monitor risks (Value at Risk) across all portfolios.
- **StatVaR**^{TM} provides an efficient, inexpensive service to ensure compliance with the UCITS III risk reporting regulations in every country in Europe.
- **StatPro Fixed Income Attribution** offers a richer performance analysis of absolute or relative fixed income strategies than any other system.
- **StatPro Performance & Attribution** provides analysis for equity and balanced portfolios combined with unparalleled speed and scalability.
- **StatPro Composites** is the industry leader in composite management for GIPS compliance. It is now available in a web edition with a workflow module.
- **StatPro Portfolio Compliance** combines a powerful object-based rules engine and a breach management module. It supports all regulatory requirements, client mandates, and in-house rules in a single consistent infrastructure.
- **StatPro Enterprise Reporting** is a sophisticated, flexible solution for investment reporting and web publishing.

System: Linedata
Vendor: Linedata Services
Overview

Linedata Services delivers global software solutions for asset management. Linedata Services' asset management offering is a complete set of software products, spanning front to back office. The solutions address the specific requirements of mutual and institutional funds, alternative funds and fund administrators.

Front Office Solutions

- LongView Trading is a fully integrated front-office trade order management solution for global buy-side institutions, supporting the business requirements and workflows of portfolio managers, traders, and compliance officers. LongView Trading offers advanced portfolio modelling, order generation, electronic trading, and compliance functionality. By providing seamless integration to hundreds of trading destinations globally, LongView Trading simplifies and automates the trade process.
- Linedata Compliance is a multi-user compliance solution for global buy-side institutions that supports the business requirements and workflows of compliance officers, portfolio managers and traders. Linedata Compliance provides advanced compliance testing and reporting for all aspects of a firm's compliance needs. It is available as a stand-alone compliance system, or it can be fully integrated with Linedata's LongView Trading solution.

Fund Accounting Solutions

- Linedata's best-of-breed fund accounting systems provide global coverage for all geographical regions and jurisdictions.
- Linedata offers a complete back-office investment management, accounting, portfolio valuation and investment reporting solution for all types of funds and all sizes of institution. Centred on its core, real-time, multi-currency accounting system, the system manages stock positions, generates, records and accounts for all investment transactions and calculates accurate NAVs and prices for multi-class collective investment funds. A high level of automation provides greater operational efficiencies as customers can, to a large extent, operate the solution hands-off.

Transfer Agency Solutions

- Linedata's transfer agency, shareholder record-keeping systems cover all geographical regions.
- Linedata offers an adaptable, scalable solution for collective investment fund providers of all sizes. It provides a flexible framework for defining new products and terms of business, and handles all processing from dealing to box management. Using modern, industry-standard technology, plus XML connectivity, not only improves performance but maximises Straight Through Processing (STP) processing and achieves greater cost-efficiency, leaving the investment fund provider to focus on managing customer relationships, and on handling and exception items. These and other features make the system a flexible, cost-efficient and functionality-rich software solution in the retail fund/transfer agency market.

Vendor: DST International (DSTi)
System: DSTi Investment Management Solutions
Overview

DSTi offers a comprehensive suite of technology solutions for the global investment management community. Its front-, middle- and back-office functionality handles multi-currency portfolios for both institutional and retail markets. The suite of products can be used either as stand-alone applications or brought together in flexible combinations according to specific needs.

Products

▓ DSTi's Derivatives Solutions – A unique software platform that manages the entire life cycle of modelling, pricing, dealing and administration of derivatives. It enables fund management teams to create and exploit a potentially limitless number of instruments, without the need to replace existing IT systems.

▓ DSTi's Front Office Solutions – Real-time position keeping with a comprehensive and sophisticated investment data model and leading-edge messaging tools.

▓ DSTi's Investment Accounting Solutions – A complete and fully integrated suite of rich investment accounting applications.

▓ DSTi's Investment Data Solutions – Market-leading, real-time, active investment data management and applications that integrate across the entire enterprise.

▓ DSTi's Performance and Risk Solutions – Complete risk and performance management systems that are integrated, but also available separately with Fixed Income Attribution.

Other notable systems and their respective vendors include the following.

Systems	Vendor	Brief Description
Dimensions	Simcorp	Flexible solutions, which fully support true straight-through processing for front, middle and back offices, across all instrument classes. Used by fund/investment managers, and fund administrators for portfolio management and portfolio optimisation.
Portia	Thomson Financial	Provides investment management firms with the powerful, flexible tools needed for management of the daily transaction activity of their portfolios and reporting of that activity to management, clients and regulators.
APX	Advent Software Inc.	Automates all phases of the investment management process from marketing and client service to reporting, while providing access to data and built-in features for operational compliance.
Basis Point	Pendo Systems	Used for managing investment trading and operations from the front office through to the back office.

Funds Open Architect	Swiss risk financial systems	Open architecture that manages the diversity of messages, business processes and communications flows in the investment management industry.
Knowledge – Investment Management	Reuters	Information and analytics tool for investment managers. Information provided includes market views, industry views, fixed income and corporate credit data.
Socrates+	Microgen	Automates the calculation of performance and attribution analysis from receipt of data through calculation to report production.
Traders Console	Eze Castle Software	Real-time, multi-asset class, multi-strategy Order Management System (OMS) that allows users to monitor and analyse portfolios, route orders, receive executions and monitor cash balances.
Value	Sophis	Cross-asset integrated front to back application dedicated to the buy-side while providing sell-side level financial and technological capabilities with the user-friendliness, connectivity and ease of implementation required by the buy-side.
Calypso Asset Management	Calypso	Provides a common platform for all capital management products traded by an asset manager, and integrated risk dashboards with the information for a fund manager.
Eagle PT-Plus	Eagle Investment Systems LLC	Packaged partnership and tax accounting, performance measurement and reporting solution designed to meet the complex needs of the alternative investment community.
Portfolio Order Management System (POMS)	Bloomberg locations.	Connects fund managers to dealers in real time at multiple Decision-support analytics and modelling tools enable fully informed investment decisions to be made by the fund manager.

Key market trends that affect Investment Managers and Solutions Providers

The asset management landscape is complex. Advances in information technology have altered securities trading. On the flipside, developments in ever more sophisticated instruments, such as derivatives, impact the buy-side's technology needs today and will continue to do so. There are also many external compliance issues which influence developments, such as market-specific regulations (the Markets in Financial Instruments Directive (MiFID) is a key driver in Europe at the moment; Reg NMS in the US). Some of the key issues are discussed below using Charles River IMS as a case study of how systems vendors are addressing these issues.

Execution Management/ Best Execution

Best execution is a key issue in asset management today. Execution management systems (EMS) facilitate best execution through their real-time market data, availability of pre-trade analysis, and electronic connectivity to multiple trading venues. Charles River IMS includes EMS functionality.

A trader using the Charles River Trader module has the ability to analyse trades, view the market in real time, and reach multiple trading venues and tools such as Direct Market Access (DMA), Electronic Communication Networks (ECN), Alternative Trading Systems (ATS) and over 20 different sources of algorithmic trading. Charles River combines its core software with a web of strategic partnerships with brokers and other trade execution venues, enabling asset managers to execute trades in the most efficient and cost-effective way possible whilst accessing obscure liquidity pools.

Growth in Buy-Side Derivative Trading

Traditionally asset managers have traded vanilla instruments such as stocks, bonds, and currency. However, increasingly, in order to maximise returns, manage exposure, and achieve alpha, they are trading more complex instruments, such as multi-leg rate and credit derivative instruments such as credit default swaps. Initially driven by the hedge fund segment, this approach to managing a portfolio has become a mainstream practice.

This is a key area of growth for Charles River Development; it drives product development. A hallmark of the Charles River IMS is its ability to manage a wide range of different instrument types through one system.

Regulation

Charles River IMS's development for the compliance module is driven by regulatory change. MiFID is a key component in Europe that drives the need for best execution; at the most basic level this requirement is a mandate for asset managers to prove they have always made the best informed trading decisions.

Charles River continues to expand upon its global rule library to support current and future regulatory and market practice changes.

117

IT Project Types

This chapter contains a list of IT projects in Investment Management, case studies of system implementations and data requirements.

Introduction

Changes in regulations or the introduction of new regulations often trigger the inception of an IT project, be it an upgrade to an existing systems to accommodate the requirements of the new regulations, or the replacement of an existing system. Other triggers include mergers and acquisitions, moves, expansion and restructuring.

The "business" usually sponsors business-critical IT projects and "IT" acts as the implementer of the projects. IT projects have to be executed by a team that is a mix of IT and business staff, hence the need for the understanding of IT by the business and vice versa.

Common Types of IT Projects

Some common types of IT projects are:

- change management programmes
- business process reengineering projects
- implementation of new trading systems
- upgrades to existing trading systems
- implementation of risk management systems
- development of interfaces to systems
- integration of in-house systems to application service providers (ASPs)
- implementing trade data warehousing
- implementation of reporting systems
- data migration
- implementation of CRM systems
- implementation of ERP systems.

Others are:

- systems cutover
- implementation of portals
- compliance projects
- data normalisation projects
- upgrades to infrastructure
- upgrades to desktops
- desktop integration
- upgrade to fund accounting systems
- implementation of disaster recovery procedures.

119

Case Studies on IT projects in Investment Management

The following case studies[44] involve the implementation of two of LatentZero's products, Sentinel and Minerva, for two clients, BIGFUND Asset Management Group and BizInvest respectively.

BIGFUND Asset Management Group Implementation of Sentinel

BIGFUND Asset Management Group (BIGFUND AM), with €340 billion assets under management, is the global asset management arm of Grande Banque Française. One of Europe's leading asset management institutions, it offers services to insurance, financial and banking organisations, mutual funds, retirement funds and non-profit organisations.

Headquartered in Paris, BIGFUND Asset Management Group has a significant global presence, particularly in the United States where it has investment management subsidiaries involved in asset management and commercial activities.

BIGFUND AM's philosophy is to offer both a long-term commitment to its clients in line with their requirements, and to develop first-rate, innovative financial solutions that meet stringent risk management and compliance requirements. As a result, risk management is one of the company's key values.

The compliance challenge

Until recently, BIGFUND AM had suffered from the lack of an automated compliance system that would have enabled the company to achieve its goals of guaranteeing full control of risk management issues and meeting increasingly demanding regulatory and investment restrictions and more complex client mandates.

In-house risk management and compliance systems, as well as the control processes implemented within BIGFUND, were not satisfactory. There was clearly a need to have a simple and easy-to-update solution that could be integrated with new and increasingly complex investment restrictions.

Solving the problem with Capstone Sentinel

To overcome this challenge, BIGFUND AM commissioned a Request for Proposal in 2003 that was aimed at selecting the best compliance solution in the marketplace. BIGFUND AM was looking for a product that would adhere to its organisational IT processes and requirements, as well as meet the requirements of the French regulatory authority, the Autorité des Marchés Financiers (AMF), which was increasingly demanding pre-trade portfolio compliance controls.

Workshops with three short-listed providers were conducted, involving the key members of BIGFUND AM's portfolio management and compliance teams. Following these, BIGFUND AM unanimously selected Capstone Sentinel™ from LatentZero™.

---

44 Case studies supplied by LatentZero, but the names of the clients and individuals have been changed for obvious reasons.

Pierre Platini, LatentZero's key contact at BIGFUND AM, explains: *"Sentinel was by far the most robust, powerful system both in terms of integration and reliability. Its modern architecture provides web-based client access for faster implementation and easier monitoring of incidents within subsidiaries. It also gives us fast response times and has the potential to conduct pre-trade checks.*

"Faced with timing and budget pressures, Capstone Sentinel was implemented in six months, finally completing in mid-2004. The emphasis of the project implementation was on building rules as quickly as possible and importing rule narratives directly from an existing database.

"BIGFUND AM then set up a dedicated team, headed by Pierre Platini, which was committed to optimising the use of Sentinel, including monitoring all the rules in the system, and managing the rule-building, validation and control process. In order to be independent from the portfolio management team while remaining close to the compliance division, this team was called the 'Cellule Sentinel' and was integrated within the internal control department. On the other side, the detection and management of investment breaches identified by Sentinel was given to a specific team that was part of the Middle Office.

"The first mission of the 'Cellule Sentinel' was to review all investment restrictions covering the 400 portfolios that were BIGFUND AM's responsibility. These investment restrictions include AMF regulatory rules and client rules, as well as internal and client-specific mandates. The upgrade to version 4.3 of Sentinel enabled BIGFUND AM to build universal rules and substantially reduce the total number from 7,200 to 1,200.

"The LatentZero Paris office also opened around that time. This greatly enhanced the relationship with LatentZero, as they were able to deal directly with the French team who quickly understood our needs and explained them to their London colleagues much better than they could. In addition, their extensive expertise in compliance issues and fund management systems was invaluable, particularly when we upgraded to the new version or had to build specific complex rules. Because of the precise and efficient responses, and the improvements incorporated into their software upgrades, LatentZero has proven that they are definitely a first-rate software provider, well aware of full compliance requirements, especially those specific to the French market. It is important to stress the fact that this is unique for an Anglo-Saxon vendor who, at the time we first contacted them, had had no prior experience of dealing with French clients."

Results

Today, Sentinel is the only system used to manage and control rules at BIGFUND AM, including universal rules, AMF regulatory rules and client mandates. The workflow implemented by the 'Cellule Sentinel' has enhanced the importance of the compliance engine to the organisation, as well as improved fund managers' knowledge of portfolio rules.

Pierre Platini explains: *"Sentinel has been really well accepted by the fund managers. They felt they were better informed of the regulatory implications, of the way they manage funds, and had useful help to monitor their risks. The 'Cellule Sentinel' is involved very early in the validation of client and statutory*

121

rules, thus working with both sales and fund managers to rationalise constraints' writing and identify needs of specific client categories. On the other side, the 'Cellule Sentinel', while seeking the most efficient data supply system, remains the key contact for the IT teams to enable the building of new rules, such as the AMF 'Nouveau ratio d'engagement, AMF, Chapter VI'. The 'Cellule Sentinel' guides and monitors the Middle Office people in charge of managing investment breaches, and assigns them to the asset managers responsible in order to find the most appropriate solutions when specific cases occur."

Pierre believes that BIGFUND AM can be proud of the result achieved in terms of post-trade compliance. *"This is the result of strong collaboration with the LatentZero teams. BIGFUND AM was among one of the first institutions in France to commit fully to the compliance requirements using a robust and scalable solution. The result speaks for itself: Sentinel currently controls 97 per cent of all their investment restrictions. This has enabled the company to strengthen their relationships with clients, and has helped their fund managers to concentrate on fund performance."*

BizInvest Implementation of Minerva
Background
BizInvest Asset Management is Norway's largest provider of mutual funds and discretionary asset management services, with a total of NOK 540 billion assets under management. Of these, approximately NOK 470 billion represent investments funds from institutional clients, with NOK 250 billion in Norway and NOK 220 billion in Sweden.

BizInvest Asset Management is a division of Norway's biggest financial services group, which itself has total assets of more than NOK 1,200 billion. The company was established following the merger of JVb and Oslo Inc NOR in 2003, and has bases in Oslo, Stockholm, London, New York and Hong Kong.

Integrating legacy systems
Because of the merger and the company's wide geographic spread, BizInvest had a number of disparate trading systems. Each of its offices around the world had a separate order management system (OMS), which meant there were different set-ups at each desk and several interfaces to the back office, making it difficult for portfolio managers to pass an order from one desk to another. In addition, the likelihood of errors in the data being used was far greater. The net result was that the whole trading process was not running at optimum efficiency.

Sven Jonsson, Head of Global Trading at BizInvest, felt that the merger in 2003 was a turning point for the firm. "With two companies now operating as one, trading volumes naturally increased, which led to performance problems - particularly at the main dealing desk in our Stockholm office. It was clear that the firm needed a new order management system that could be rolled out globally and which would bring together all our diverse systems, integrate with their legacy systems, and, most of all, improve the efficiency of their workflows across all our trading desks."

Connectivity and usability

To select the right system, BizInvest conducted a rigorous selection process that saw an initial long list of ten products narrowed down to three for a detailed evaluation. From this shortlist, LatentZero's order management system, Minerva, was eventually selected.

Jonsson concluded that they were looking for an OMS and a supplier that would deliver against four main criteria. First of all, they were interested in a long-term relationship with their chosen partner. Then the product had to be able to integrate with different back-office systems that included SIMCorp Dimension in the back office as well as in-house developments. Thirdly, they wanted a straightforward implementation process and, finally, a reasonable price. They were very impressed by Minerva and LatentZero on all four counts.

In addition, Minerva offered JVb NOR's traders the functionality they were looking for, combined with a look and feel that users liked. It provided dealers with state-of-the-art technology that best met their requirements, including more efficient workflows and a significantly improved STP.

BizInvest also wanted connectivity to FIX, as well as other liquidity sources, in order to maintain their connections with top-rank brokers. The high level of connectivity within Minerva was a further reason for choosing it above other products on the shortlist.

Finally, BizInvest felt that Minerva would enable the company to measure performance and best execution more accurately across its global operations. Jonsson concluded that with MiFID just around the corner, it was essential that they had a system that could prepare for its arrival and support the wider move to more transparent trading practices.

However, what really clinched the deal was the experience, knowledge and attitude of LatentZero's people, and the overall feel of the company. LatentZero was clearly prepared to be flexible, and to discuss different types of partnership, so that a relationship could be developed that suited both parties. LatentZero's positive attitude, the usability of its system and the testimonials received from its very impressive client list persuaded the board that they were the right choice for JVb NOR.

Implementation

Worldwide roll-out started in September 2004 and the system went live across all desks in a staggered sequence throughout spring 2005. The initial focus was on equity trading, as this was the area that had seen the biggest problems in the existing system. However, it was important that the system could handle fixed income and foreign exchange in the longer term.

Jonsson and his team were very satisfied with the level of support offered by LatentZero throughout the implementation process. There were a couple of unexpected problems, primarily to do with the use of specific characters in the Swedish alphabet. But LatentZero helped them to overcome these and BizInvest were impressed by the way they helped find a solution to the problem.

Results

BizInvest has achieved much more efficient workflows and better performance in all its offices since implementing Minerva. They face lower operational risk and better reporting and compliance checks, which are essential in the face of MiFID and other regulations. Having data in one big database also reduces error and offers substantial benefits.

Cutting Edge Technology

One of the hottest technologies to hit the financial market scene in recent times is Service-Oriented Architecture, known in the industry along with Web Services as WS/SOA.

What is SOA?

It is quite difficult to come up with a specific definition for SOA, in fact there is no agreed-upon definition. However, an attempt/working definition is:

Service Oriented Architecture in concert with Web Services are enablers for the collaborative meshing of technologies, processes and organisational models to create new services or leverage the benefits of existing services.

A quote from Microsoft[45] complements this definition as follows:

> *"Adopting SOA is essential to deliver the business agility and IT flexibility promised by Web Services. These benefits are delivered not by just viewing service architecture from a technology perspective and the adoption of Web Service protocols, but require the creation of a Service-Oriented Environment that is based on the following key principals:*
>
> - *Service is the important concept. Web Services are the set of protocols by which Services can be published, discovered and used in a technology-neutral, standard form.*
> - *SOA is not just an architecture of services seen from a technology perspective, but the policies, practices, and frameworks by which we (Microsoft) ensure the right services are provided and consumed.*
> - *With SOA it is critical to implement processes that ensure that there are at least two different and separate processes – for provider and consumer."*

An interesting, but simplified illustration of this abstract concept using a scenario from our everyday lives is as follows.

Take, for an example, a DVD player in the living room; it offers DVD-playing

---

45 Source: www.microsoft.com/biztalk/solutions/soa/overview.mspx.

services for a collection of DVDs at a particular level of quality. However, playing the DVDs in a home cinema offers DVD-playing services as well but at a better level of quality. The DVD-playing service is akin to the Web Services that define SOA.

Adoption of SOA in Investment Management

Investment Management firms will be looking to adopt SOA in the face of business growth, demands of globalisation and regulatory changes. To this end, the need for adoption of SOA and the benefits will be discussed in this section.

Why SOA?

There is growing concern in most business sectors that their existing IT portfolios are not aligned to their business needs and aspirations. The problem is not inherent in existing functionality, but in the disconnection between disparate business-critical systems such as Customer Relationship Management (CRM) and Enterprise Resource Planning (ERP) systems and other systems such as portfolio management and fund accounting systems.

SOA addresses this problem by enabling the organisation of IT resources into a company-wide integrated solution that ensures information flow across business systems.

A typical scenario is described below.

A fictitious investment management company, Biz Global Investors, is undergoing a massive restructuring of the business in the face of increasing competition and new regulations. The Chief Information Officer (CIO) is under pressure to trim costs and deliver improved technology effectiveness.

Problem

The IT function of the firm is made up of independent groups that take decisions in isolation. These groups make deployment decisions in silos as opposed to a collaborative enterprise-wide manner. This has resulted in a range of disconnected solutions based on redundant technology.

Solution

The CIO's mandate is to support cross-organisation processes through standardisation and convergence of the technology portfolio. They decide to adopt an SOA in a new initiative across the subsidiaries and geographically distributed locations.

The following are the IT and business benefits of adopting SOA:

- An automated information transfer process allows the IT function to develop new applications, and collaborate with existing and new trading partners and customers.
- Synchronisation across business units and parties provides a "single view" of each customer while ensuring consistency and aggregation across the value chain.

125

▓ A holistic view of the business is achieved through the deployment of cross-organisation processes and acceleration of service deployment.

▓ The simplified management of distributed resources across multiple platforms leads to cost savings.

▓ The business decision-making process is enhanced as a result of access to more accurate and comprehensive information.

▓ With a more holistic enterprise, problem management and traceability becomes easier for all parties concerned and they get a snapshot of causes and effects.

According to Bearings Point, Web Services/Service-Oriented Architecture provides mechanisms to look up and find information about services and learn how to use them. A WS/SOA framework is generally built from shelf components and customised depending on the needs and capabilities of the implementing organisation.

Bearings Point also defines two types of services:

▓ Business services – that provide industry-specific, higher-level business functionalities, for example market-data feeds and stock portfolio management.

▓ Application services – that facilitate the creation of and access to business services and represent generic, non-industry-specific capabilities within a framework. Error handling and security are examples of application services.

Figure 9.1: Service-based conceptual architecture

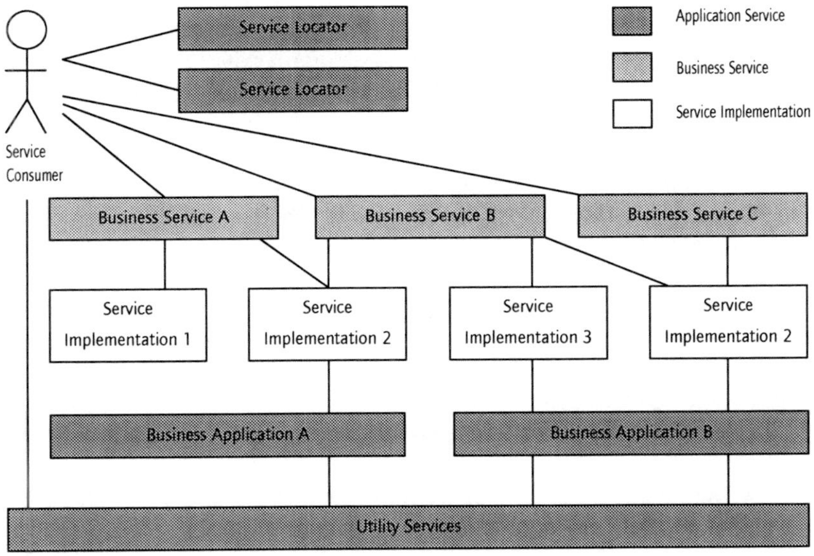

Source: Bearing Point. Reproduced with permission

Figure 9.1 shows a conceptual architecture for a service-based WS/SOA, including key terms.

According to Bearing Point, *"With this architecture, first-time service consumers look up services and get information on how to use them through the service locator. Subsequent requests can be direct, without going through the service locator. A security service governs all interactions. Services expose and organise business functionalities provided by service implementations. The service implementations are based on the capabilities of existing applications. A new service implementation could remain stand-alone or be integrated into an existing application as a new feature or an enhancement."*

An investment management firm can implement the conceptual model shown in Figure 9.1 using a variety of technologies.

Case Study: BigFund Investment Managers/Outsoz Global Investors

To elucidate the concept, a case study[46] involving an investment management company is discussed below.

BigFund Investment Managers (BIM), an investment management firm in the City of London, has an internal application for real-time stock quotes that BIM dealers use for trading. The firm has decided to enter the online trading business. To speed time-to-market and lower costs, it has chosen to outsource the required online trading application to Outsoz Global Investors (OGI). OGI would provide the web-based trading application and manage all transactions on behalf of BIM. The application would support two classes of service: "preferred customers" would get real-time stock quotes whereas "value customers" would get delayed quotes.

BIM has decided to provide its own stock quote service, which BIM will incorporate in the online trading application. Figure 9.2 illustrates the scenario.

BIM has adopted a WS/SOA framework with the goal of facilitating both in-house and outsourced application development and integration. Initially, three application services are supported: security, discovery and data access. The existing trading application already has a set of proprietary Application Programming Interfaces (APIs), which provide the foundation for the stock quotes service implementation. BIM has defined the stock quotes business service to provide real-time or delayed quotes and to be implemented as a Web Service. On the back end, the trading application retrieves information related to stock symbols from a database with the help of the data access application service. An external provider provides market data using a legacy interface that does not yet participate in the framework.

This example exemplifies several reasons for implementing SOA including:

▓ The adoption of WS/SOA supplements and builds upon existing stock quotes and back-end applications, which can be reused.

46 Case study was constructed by extrapolating "BigTraderCompany and SmallTraderCompany" case study from Bearing Point's Financial Services Journal Vol. 1 Issue 1.

Figure 9.2 BigFund Investment Managers/Outsoz Global Investors use case and logical view

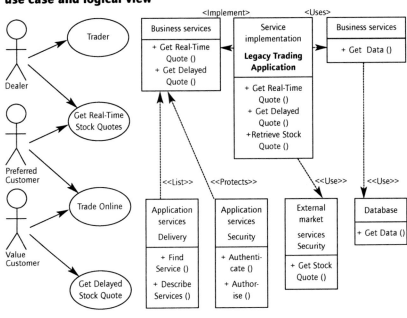

Source: Bearing Point. Reproduced with permission

■ Minimisation of the impact of new services, which can be rolled out in a phase-wise manner, on the enterprise and its partners.

Data Requirements

Data requirements of investment management firms vary from firm to firm and internally from department to department. Fund managers have different data requirement to compliance officers, equity fund managers have different requirements to currency fund managers.

Investment managers typically choose to source their data from different vendors depending upon the market in which they are investing. Hence for mainstream securities they may choose to source data from exchanges (via Reuters or Bloomberg or other vendor) while data for less commonly traded securities is sourced directly from brokers specialising in the markets in question. In modern times, electronic data feeds are essential for fund managers' portfolio analysis systems. These securities data feeds are indexed by one or more familiar and unique security codes so that they can be used by these systems. The most widely used codes are:

■ International Security Identification Number (ISIN), described in Chapter 2 and the preferred code for bonds;

■ Stock Exchange Daily Official List (SEDOL).[47] This is a list of codes for equities in general;

■ Series of codes from the major vendors, DataStream, Reuters and Bloomberg, which are unique to their systems;

■ Exchange Ticker used in conjunction with exchange and date to uniquely identify a security.

In investment management firms, the investment accounting systems generally hold the main record of investment activity and positions for client funds. The data held in these systems is cascaded throughout the organisation including the front office. As a result, the data requirements for the front office include:

■ Data definition with a view to linking corporate action data, e.g. dividend to the stocks that generate them.

■ Static data definition with a view to linking a fund and securities held by other funds.

■ Economic research data from vendors such as Bloomberg to enable analysts to identify the link between economic factors like interest rates and exchange rates that affect prices of securities.

The following table shows examples of data that investment managers manning different desks require:

Desk	Data Type
Equity Management	Stock level indices
	Security classification (market, currency etc.)
	Security-specific data (price, earnings, beta etc.)
	Index constituent flag
	Price
	Number of shares in issue
	Indexed security news service
Currency Management	Spot rates
	Cross rates
	Interest rates
Fixed Interest Management	Stock level indices
	Index constituent flag
	Gross price
	Prior charge capital/amount outstanding

47 SEDOL is a list of security identifiers used in the United Kingdom and Ireland for clearing purposes. The numbers are assigned by the London Stock Exchange, on request by the security issuer. SEDOLs serve as the National Securities Identifying Number (NSIN) for all securities issued in the United Kingdom and it is therefore part of the security's ISIN as well.

10

Commonly Used Terms in Investment Management

This chapter lists the terminology commonly used in the industry that IT professionals will come across in the course of the business day in investment management firms.

Introduction

Investment managers have jargon that is unique to their sector and other terms that are used generally in the financial services sector which are second nature to them. However, the discerning IT professional in investment management needs to be familiar with this jargon to ensure that they can communicate freely with the business staff and also to build and support business applications.

Against this backdrop, the following terms have been compiled to familiarise readers with the terminology of the industry. It should be noted that this is not an exhaustive list but is deemed sufficient for the context of this publication. Further searches can be carried out on the Internet (**www.bizle.biz**) or in textbooks and journals for other terms not covered in this section.

List of Terms[48]

Accumulation units/shares. With this type of unit/share, any income earned remains accumulated within the price of your unit/share, increasing the value of your holding.

Active managed funds. Funds which aim to outperform a benchmark index, such as the FTSE 100. The aim is for the fund manager to manage the fund's investments in such a way that the fund will generate better returns than you might receive in a passive managed fund.

Authorised Corporate Director (ACD). The term used to describe the manager of an OEIC fund. An ACD has the same role and responsibilities as their unit trust equivalents, known as the fund manager.

Annual management charge (AMC). A fee paid to the fund manager once a year which covers the cost of investment management and administration. It is normally 0.75%–1.5% per annum and is charged to the fund.

Annual report. Includes details of the fund's investments and how it has performed with more general financial information relating to the fund. It is sent to you by your fund manager at the end of each financial year.

Assets. Usually stocks and shares, fixed interest securities or cash, these are the "building blocks" in which a fund invests.

Asset allocation. A term to describe how your money is invested. In most cases, the fund manager will spread money across a range of different assets and companies in order to diversify your holdings and help to spread risk.

Authorised fund. A unit trust or OEIC that is authorised by the Financial Services Authority (FSA) for promotion to the general public in the UK. All unit trusts and OEICs which are on sale to a retail investor in the UK are authorised by the FSA.

48 List of terms supplied by Investment Management Association.

Balanced fund. A type of fund which restricts its investment in equities to a maximum of 85% of the fund's holdings in order to invest in other types of investments such as bonds. This type of fund aims to benefit from the performance of its bond investments when equities are not performing well and vice versa.

Benchmark index. A stock market index, such as the FTSE 100, which is used to measure the overall performance of the shares that are contained within it. Fund managers try to outperform any gains made by their fund's benchmark index.

Bid price. Some unit trusts have separate prices for buying and selling units. The bid price is the selling price of your units.

Bid/Offer spread. For dual-priced unit trusts, this is the percentage difference between the buying and selling prices of your units. The buying or offer price is normally higher than the selling or bid price as it will include an initial charge to be paid to the fund manager for setting up and administering your units.

Blue chip. Large well-established companies which are generally considered to be stable. In the UK, such British companies are usually listed on the FTSE 100 index.

Bonds. Also known as fixed interest securities, bonds are investments which pay a fixed rate of interest and have a fixed term. Governments or companies may issue them. Those issued by Governments are known as gilts. Not to be confused with investment bonds issued for individual investors, usually by insurance companies.

Buy side. Investing institutions such as mutual funds, pension funds and insurance firms that tend to buy large portions of securities for money-management purposes.

Cancellation price. For dual-priced unit trusts, this is the lowest possible price at which an investor can sell units back to the manager under FSA regulations. It excludes exit charges. The cancellation price represents the proceeds the fund would receive if the fund's assets were sold.

Capital. The amount of money you initially put into your savings or investments before it receives any interest or capital growth. In a fund, "capital" can also refer to the assets held by the fund excluding any income the fund may receive.

Capital gains tax. Tax paid to the Inland Revenue on any increase in the value of your savings or investments. The tax is payable on the capital profits you make when you sell your units/shares. There is an annual exemption limit; for the current tax year (2007) this is £8,200.

Capital growth. The increase in the value of your investment, excluding any income you have received from it.

Cash. In saving and investment terms, refers to a bank or building society deposit account in which your capital is secure.

Cash funds. Alternative name for money market funds.

CAT standards. Voluntary standards introduced by the Government which can be applied to a number of products including ISAs. CAT stands for Charges, Access and Terms but does not guarantee performance or suitability of the fund.

Cautious managed fund. A type of fund which restricts its investment in equities to a maximum of 60% of the fund's holdings in order to invest in other types of investments such as cash and bonds. This type of fund is considered to be more "cautious" than funds which invest more of their holdings in equities, as more of its portfolios are diversified across less risky investments in cash and bonds.

Closed-ended funds. Unlike unit trusts and OEICs which are open-ended, these are funds which only have a predetermined number of units/shares in issue at any time. The price of units/shares in such funds, which include Investment Trusts, will fluctuate according to investor demand rather than simply because of changes in the value of their underlying assets.

Collective investment schemes. Funds which pool investors' money and invest on their behalf. This term refers to unit trusts and OEICs.

Compounding. The process by which your investment grows in value over time with reinvested interest or dividends.

Corporate bonds. Fixed interest securities issued by public companies.

Creation price. For dual-priced unit trusts this is the highest possible price at which an investor can buy units from the manager under FSA regulations. The initial charge is not included. The creation price represents the cost of buying the fund's assets.

Credit ratings. Ratings provided by specialist credit agencies which assess the likelihood of companies being able to meet their financial obligations. Ratings range from AAA (the most secure) to D (the least secure); the greater the credit risk the lower the rating.

Credit risk. Usually used when referring to investment in bonds, credit ratings agencies estimate the likelihood that the issuer of the bond will not be able to keep up your interest payments or repay your capital at the end of the holding period. "Triple A" or "investment grade rated" are considered to be the lowest credit risk while non-investment grade, also known as junk bonds and rated triple B–D, are the highest credit risk.

Currency risk. When the manager buys investments in currencies other than Sterling, there is a risk that the value of those investments will change owing to changes in currency exchange rates.

Current yield. See running yield.

Custodian. Usually a major banking group, the custodian is appointed by the fund's trustee or depositary to safeguard the fund's assets.

Default risk. The risk that a company may not be able to pay you back the money you have invested.

133

Deposit account. A bank or building society account which earns a steady rate of interest and in which your original capital is secure. The interest rates paid vary depending on the length of time you are prepared to lock your money away for.

Depositary. Responsible for overseeing the fund manager's activities in relation to an OEIC. Usually a large bank, the depositary must be independent of the fund manager where the fund is authorised by the Financial Services Authority. It acts in the interests of the investors, owning the investments in the fund on their behalf. It also ensures that the fund is invested according to its investment objectives and that the manager complies with the regulations. The unit trust equivalent is known as the trustee.

Derivatives. A general term for futures and options.

Discount broker. A service provided by an intermediary where no advice is taken. Also known as an "execution only" service, the broker will buy a product on behalf of an investor after the investor has chosen which product they would like to purchase. Discount brokers usually waive or discount the initial charge, as no advice has been provided. This service is often available by post and rather than pay commission you are charged a one-off transaction charge.

Distributions. Income paid out from a unit trust or OEIC in the form of interest or dividends.

Diversification. A term used to describe the spreading of risk by investing in a number of different companies and assets. Doing so will mean that you won't have all of your eggs in one basket.

Dividends. Income paid on shares out of company profits.

Dividend distributions. Income paid out by unit trusts and OEICs that invest mainly in equities.

Dual pricing. Dual-priced funds have an offer price at which you buy, and a lower bid price, at which you sell. The difference between the two prices is known as the bid/offer spread. The buying price is normally higher than the selling price as this includes the initial charge to be paid to the fund manager.

Equities. Shares in a company (see also stocks and shares).

Equity exposure. Usually expressed in percentage form. This illustrates the proportion of a fund which is invested in stocks and shares (equities).

Ethical funds. Also known as Socially Responsible Investments (SRIs). These funds aim to avoid investing in activities which may be harmful to society, such as tobacco production or child labour. Some funds also aim to actively invest in companies which promote ethical policies such as recycling.

Ex-dividend (xd). For a fund, the period between its accounting date and when it pays out its income. If you buy a unit trust in this period you do not get the income, but if you sell you do.

Exempt funds. Refers to funds that are only open to institutional investors which are exempt from paying capital gains tax, such as pension funds and charities.

Exit charge. Also known as redemption charge. A charge taken by the managers of some funds when you sell units. In many cases, the charge will only be applied if you sell within, say, five years. Exit charges are usually applied instead of, rather than in addition to, an initial charge.

Expected income yield. An estimate of the income that you might earn in the coming year if you bought units at the current price.

Expenses charged to capital. Expenses incurred by the fund can either be taken out of the income received by the fund or from the fund's capital. Charging expenses to capital will increase the amount that can be paid out to investors as distributions but will reduce the capital value of the fund.

Fact find. A process undertaken by independent financial advisers (IFAs) to establish the financial position, investment goals and attitude to risk of their clients to ensure that suitable advice is given.

Fair value pricing. This is the manager's best estimate of the value of one or more securities at the valuation point of the fund, with the intention of producing a "fairer" dealing price where there is doubt over the validity of those prices.

Financial Ombudsman Service (FOS). Customers with a complaint against a financial services firm can make a complaint to the FOS who will investigate on their behalf. If the company no longer exists or has become insolvent you should contact the Financial Services Compensation Scheme (FSCS).

Financial Services and Markets Act 2000. The Act of Parliament which gave the Financial Services Authority its regulatory powers from 2001. These powers include supervision of the scope of regulated activities, the control of financial promotion, and the authority to regulate, investigate and discipline the financial services industry.

Financial Services Compensation Scheme (FSCS). This scheme exists for claims against an authorised financial services company when it is unable to pay claims against it as it is insolvent or no longer trading. For companies still in business, claims must be taken to the Financial Ombudsman Service.

Fixed interest securities. Provide regular, fixed, interest payments and are issued by companies and governments. They include gilts and bonds.

Forward pricing. This is the most common method of pricing authorised funds. Once the manager has received your instruction to buy or sell units, the price of those units will be determined at the next valuation point of the fund.

Free Standing Additional Voluntary Contribution (FSAVC) schemes. These permit people who are part of a company pension scheme to make additional contributions to a separate stand-alone scheme that can continue when you change employer.

FTSE 100 Index. British index on the London Stock Exchange of leading 100 UK Companies.

FTSE 250 Index. British index on the London Stock Exchange of the largest 250 companies by market capitalisation after those listed on the FTSE 100.

FTSE All Share Index. British index on the London Stock Exchange of all UK listed companies. Incorporates companies from the FTSE 100, FTSE 250 and FTSE Small Cap indices.

FTSE Small Cap Index. British index of the smallest companies by market capitalisation.

Fund manager. Manages the unit trust in accordance with the fund's objectives and decides which assets to hold in order to meet those objectives. In an OEIC the manager is referred to as the Authorised Corporate Director (ACD).

Fund of funds. Funds of funds are designed to increase diversification by investing in other funds.

Futures. Agreement to buy or sell a fixed amount of a particular asset at a fixed future date and a fixed price.

Gilts. Bonds issued by the UK Government. Also known as gilt-edged securities. Along with bonds, can be referred to as fixed interest securities.

Gearing. The amount a fund can "gear" is the amount it can borrow in order to invest. In unit trusts and OEICs, borrowing is limited to 10% of the fund's value and is usually for the purpose of managing cash flow rather than to increase the fund's investment exposure.

Gross income. Dividends and interest paid out to you before income tax has been deducted.

Gross redemption yield. Usually used in bond investments. This yield seeks to indicate the total return you might receive from both income and capital growth (or loss) if you hold your investment over a ten-year period.

Guaranteed fund. This is where a fund manager promises to provide a specific minimum return, backed by a legally enforceable arrangement with a third party to guarantee that promise.

Hedge funds. A fund which uses an assortment of trading techniques and instruments to meet an objective of providing positive investment returns irrespective of the performance of stock markets.

Historic pricing. Where the price at which you buy or sell your units/shares is calculated at the last valuation point, i.e. the fund manager uses the price set before they received your instructions.

ICVC. Investment Company with Variable Capital. Another term used to describe an OEIC. This term is used rarely but you may come across it in formal documents relating to an OEIC.

Income. The return on your investment that arises from dividends and interest earned by the fund.

Income tax. A tax payable to the Inland Revenue on any income you receive whether it is wages or income from investments and savings. Different rates of income tax apply; the one you pay depends on how much money you have coming in.

Income units/shares. This type of unit/share pays out to you on set dates each year any interest or dividends your investment makes.

Index/indices. A grouping of shares or fixed interest securities on the stock market which are often similar in size or represent similar industries. For example, the FTSE 100 index represents the largest 100 UK companies by market capitalisation.

Index tracking funds. Index tracking funds aim to mirror the progress of a stock market index, e.g. the FTSE 100, by buying and selling shares in the same proportions as represented on the index. These are also sometimes called tracker funds or index funds.

Inflation. A general rise in the level of prices on the high street. This is measured by the retail price index.

Inflation risk. The risk to your savings caused by rising inflation. If inflation rises but interest on your savings doesn't keep up, it can reduce the spending power of your money. A £1 coin will always be worth £1, but what you can buy with that coin will reduce with increased inflation.

Initial charge. A charge that is paid to the fund manager, when you invest, to cover their expenses, such as commission, advertising, administration and dealing costs.

Institutional investor. Institutions which invest, such as company pension schemes, as opposed to private individuals.

Instrument of Incorporation. This document forms the legal constitution for an OEIC fund and dictates much of how the fund will operate. The unit trust equivalent is known as the Trust Deed.

Interest. An amount, in percentage form, which a bank or building society will credit to you if you save with it in a deposit/savings account. The amount paid to you will be a percentage of whatever capital you have in your account. Gilts and bonds also pay income in the form of interest.

Interest distributions. Income paid out by unit trusts and OEICs that invest predominantly in gilts and bonds.

Intermediary. When buying a financial product you may not want to buy from the fund management company directly but go to a third party who may be able to offer you advice or a discount. These third parties are known as intermediaries and include banks, building societies and independent financial advisers.

Investment funds. A general term for unit trusts and OEICs.

Investment grade bonds. These bonds have a low risk of the company that issued the bonds being unable to repay them. The most secure forms are known as "triple A" bonds. (See credit ratings).

Investment trusts. Similar to unit trusts in that they provide a means of pooling your investment but with a different structure and governed by different regulations. They are closed ended funds and public listed companies whose shares are traded on the London Stock Exchange.

Key features document. This document must be offered to an investor before or at the point of purchase. It summarises key information about the fund and is less detailed than the prospectus. It provides additional information to the prospectus such as information on risk and an illustration of the effects of charges both to the investor and the fund.

Life insurance products. Products which guarantee that a sum of money will be paid out to you after a set term or upon death.

Limited redemption funds. Funds which restrict when you can cash in your investment, usually by having only set redemption dates.

Market capitalisation. The value of a company obtained by multiplying the number of its issued shares by their market price.

Market risk. Investing in the stock market means that you can benefit from its growth potential. However, there is also a risk (market risk) that you could lose your money should the stock market in which you have invested fall in value.

Money market funds. These invest in cash investments, such as bank deposits. Often referred to as "cash funds", they offer higher returns than a building society account but still have the same level of security.

Multimanager funds. Multimanager funds are designed to increase diversification by a Manager of Managers outsourcing a pool of money for investment to appointed managers.

Net income. Dividends and interest paid out to you after income tax has been deducted.

Non-investment-grade bonds. These bonds have a high risk of the company that issued the bonds being unable to repay them. They are lower-rated bonds on the share index, with a poor credit rating often as low as D. They are sometimes referred to as "junk bonds".

OEICs. Open ended investment companies. These are very similar to unit trusts, but are constituted as companies rather than trusts. They are the established structure in many other European countries and are usually single priced.

Offer price. Some unit trusts have separate prices for buying and selling units. The offer price is the one at which you buy units and is usually higher than the bid price as it includes an initial charge.

Open-ended fund. Funds such as unit trusts and OEICs which expand and contract by issuing or cancelling units/shares, depending upon demand.

Options. Provide the opportunity (a "right" rather than an obligation) for the buyer to purchase or sell a certain number of shares, at a future date and a known price.

Passive managed fund. Passive managed funds aim to mirror the progress of a stock market index, e.g. the FTSE 100, by buying and selling shares in the same proportions as represented on the index. These are also sometimes called tracker funds or index (tracker) funds.

Portfolio. Refers to investment holdings. It can either refer to the holdings within a particular fund or the range of investments held by an individual investor.

Pound cost averaging. Investing on a regular basis can iron out stock market fluctuations and can help you to avoid investing all of your money when the market is at its peak. Saving regularly enables you to buy more shares when the market and prices are low and less when the market and prices are high. Over time the cost of your units will even out and it is likely that you will end up paying below average prices for your units. This is known as pound cost averaging.

Preference shares. These are similar to bonds in that they usually pay a fixed rate of income. However, they pay it as a dividend rather than interest and are subject to the issuing company making sufficient profits.

Prospectus. Offered to an investor before the point of purchasing units/shares. This document formally sets out further detail on aspects covered in the instrument of incorporation or trust deed such as charges, distribution dates and investment policy but in a less legalistic way. For unit trusts it is sometimes known as the Scheme Particulars.

Protected funds. Funds other than money market (cash) funds which aim to provide a return of a minimum amount of capital back to the investor, with the potential for some growth. Unlike guaranteed funds, they do not back their promise with a guarantee.

Provider. A financial company, in the case of unit trusts and OEICs a fund management company, which provides financial products to members of the public.

Retail investor. Term referring to members of the general investing public.

Return. The amount of income, capital growth or both that is generated by your investment.

Risk profile. This relates to how much risk you are prepared to take with your money. Generally the more risk you take, the higher the potential gain but the more likely it is that you could lose some or all of your capital. Your risk profile may depend on your financial circumstances, as some people are able to take more risk than others. If you are unsure of your risk profile you should contact an independent financial adviser for assistance before making an investment.

Running yield. Also known as income yield. The amount of income generated by a bond or gilt fund at the current time.

Sectors. Unit trusts and OEICs are divided into a variety of categories, known as sectors, to keep together funds of a similar type so that investors can compare funds with similar objectives and investment strategies. Categories include "Money market" funds, "European" funds, "North American" funds etc.

Securities. Another name for documented investments such as stocks, shares and bonds.

Sell side. The retail brokers and research departments that sell securities and make recommendations for brokerage firms' customers.

Shares. The name given to a part of a company owned by an investor – the investor buys shares in the company. It is also used to describe the OEIC equivalent of a unit.

Single pricing. OEICs and some unit trusts have a single price at which investors both buy and sell. The initial charge is shown separately and is charged in addition to the unit/share price.

Socially responsible investment funds. See ethical funds.

Stocks and shares. Also known as equities, this is the name given to a part of a company owned by an investor.

Total expense ratio. Provides investors with a clearer picture of the total annual costs for running a unit trust or OEIC. It consists principally of the manager's annual charge, but also includes the costs for other services paid for by the fund, such as the fees paid to the trustee/depositary, custodian, auditors and registrar.

Tracker funds. Tracker funds aim to mirror the progress of a stock market index, e.g. the FTSE 100, by buying and selling shares in the same proportions as represented on the index. These are also sometimes called index (tracker) funds or passive managed funds.

Trust deed. This document establishes the legal constitution, structure and organisation of a unit trust. The OEIC equivalent is known as an instrument of corporation.

Trustee. Responsible for overseeing the fund manager's activities in relation to a unit trust. Usually a large bank, the trustee must be independent of the fund manager where the fund is authorised by the Financial Services Authority. It acts in the interests of the investors, owning the investments in the fund on their behalf. It also ensures the fund is invested according to its investment objectives and that the manager complies with the regulations. The OEIC equivalent is known as the depositary.

Units. Unit trusts are divided into "units" of equal value; therefore an investor buys units in the unit trust. The OEIC equivalent is known as a share.

Unit-linked policies. These are insurance products where you pay a premium which is then invested in a fund holding a range of assets, usually including equities and fixed interest securities. Part of the premium paid pays for life assurance. Unit-linked policies are similar to with-profits products but do not invest in as many assets.

Unit trust. Private individuals pool their contributions with others, which combine to form a large fund. The fund invests in a spread of different assets to minimise the risk of loss. Also known as collective/pooled investments or investment funds. Unit trusts are usually dual priced although some can be single priced.

Valuation point. The name given to the time of day that unit trusts or OEICs are valued and then priced.

Warrants. A security that offers the owner the right to purchase the shares of a company at a fixed date, usually at a fixed price.

With profits. A with-profits fund is a pooled insurance product. With-profits funds pool together premiums paid by a number of investors, which the insurance company then invests in a very wide range of assets. (See also unit-linked policies).

Yield. The amount of income generated by a fund's investments in relation to the price. Equity funds will quote net (after tax and charges). Fixed interest securities will quote gross.

Zero dividend preference shares. Preference shares which do not pay out dividends but instead pay out a predetermined amount at the end of the investment period.

Methodologies, Skills and Tools

This chapter covers the methodologies, methods used and skills required to work in investment management.

Introduction

There is a myriad of methodologies, skills and tools used in the IT industry, but investment management firms and the financial services industry in general appear to standardise on specific tools. These will be discussed in this section as will the specific skills that are required to carry out particular duties for projects in investment management firms.

Methodologies

In software engineering and project management, "methodology" is often used to refer to a codified set of recommended practices, sometimes accompanied by training materials, formal educational programmes, worksheets and diagramming tools. In investment management, the best methodologies are employed to ensure that business-critical systems are built to a sufficient level of quality as required by the activities carried out in the industry.

Capability Maturity Model (CMM)

The Capability Maturity Model (CMM) is a way to develop and refine an organisation's processes. It was developed by the Software Engineering Institute at Carnegie Mellon University in Pittsburgh. The first CMM was for the purpose of developing and refining software development processes. The latest version (1.2) of Capability Maturity Model Integration (CMMI) contains 22 key process areas indicating the aspects of product development that are to be covered by company processes. The method by which a company chooses to adopt CMMI is called a representation. Both the staged representation and the continuous representation contain all 22 process areas. The previous version of CMMI (Ver1.1) had 25 process areas.

A maturity model is a structured collection of elements that describe characteristics of effective processes. It is a layered framework providing a progression to the discipline needed to engage in continuous improvement, while the key processes mentioned above identify a cluster of related activities that, when performed collectively, achieve a set of goals considered important. The goals of a key process area summarise the states that must exist for that key process area to have been implemented in an effective and lasting way. The extent to which the goals have been accomplished is an indicator of how much capability the organisation has established at that maturity level. The goals signify the scope, boundaries and intent of each key process area.

There are five levels of CMM that an organisation can achieve and they are as follows:

■ Level 1 – Initial: at this level, processes are usually ad hoc and the organisation usually does not provide a stable environment. Success in these organisations depends on the competence and heroics of the people in the organisation and not on the use of proven processes.

143

- Level 2 – Repeatable: at this level, software development successes are repeatable. The processes may not repeat for all the projects in the organisation.
- Level 3 – Defined: the organisation's set of standard processes, which are the basis for level 3, are established and improved over time. These standard processes are used to establish consistency across the organisation. Projects establish their defined processes by the organisation's set of standard processes according to tailoring guidelines.
- Level 4 – Quantitatively managed: using precise measurements, management can effectively control the software development effort. In particular, management can identify ways to adjust and adapt the process to particular projects without measurable losses of quality or deviations from specifications. Organisations at this level set quantitative quality goals for both software process and software maintenance.
- Level 5 – Optimising: maturity level 5 focuses on continually improving process performance through both incremental and innovative technological improvements. Quantitative process-improvement objectives for the organisation are established, continually revised to reflect changing business objectives, and used as criteria in managing process improvement.

V-Model

The V-model is a graphical representation of the system development life cycle. It summarises the main steps to be taken in conjunction with the corresponding deliverables during the life cycle.

Figure 11.1 V-Model

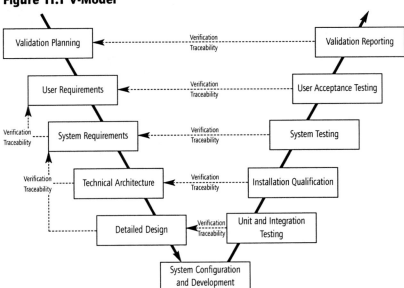

Source: Wikipedia

The left side of the V shows the specification stream where the system specifications are defined, while the right side of the V represents the testing stream where the systems are being tested (against the specifications defined on the left side). The base of the V, where the sides meet, represents the development stream.

RUP

The Rational Unified Process (RUP) is an iterative software development process created by the Rational Software Corporation, now a division of IBM. RUP is not a single concrete prescriptive process but rather an adaptable process framework. As such, RUP describes how to develop software effectively using proven techniques. While RUP encompasses a large number of different activities, it is also intended to be tailored, in the sense of selecting the development processes appropriate to a particular software project or development organisation. RUP is recognised as being particularly applicable to larger software development teams working on large projects.

Figure 11.2 RUP

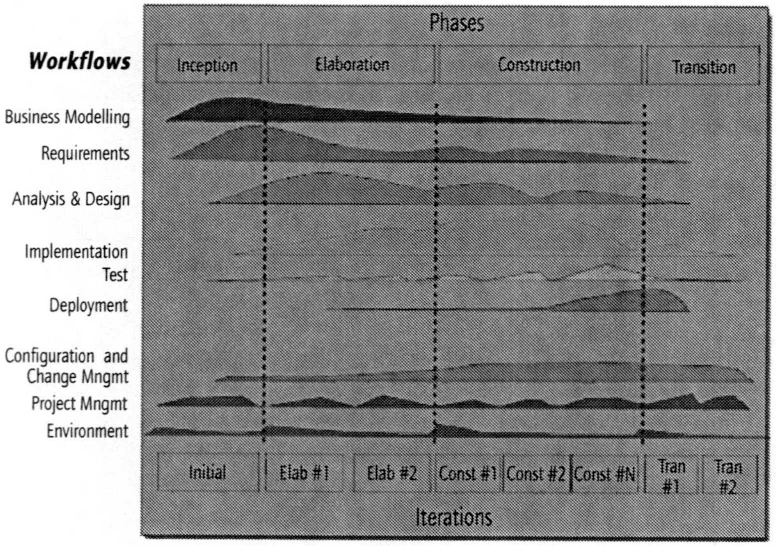

Source: Rational Software

Using RUP, software product life cycles are broken into individual development cycles. These cycles are further broken into their main components, called phases. In RUP, these phases are termed as:

- inception phase
- elaboration phase

- construction phase
- transition phase.

Phases are composed of iterations. Iterations are timeboxes; iterations have deadlines while phases have objectives.

PRINCE 2

Prince stands for Projects in Controlled Environments. Prince 2 is the latest version of Prince, released in 1996, and is a project management methodology for the organisation, management and control of projects.

Figure 11.3 Prince 2

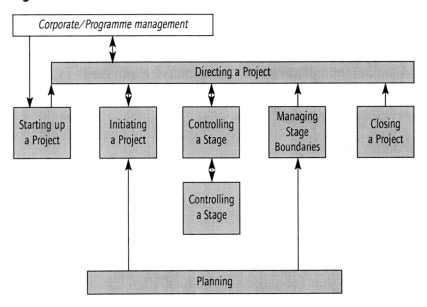

Source: Wikipedia

The diagram above shows Prince 2 processes. The arrows symbolise flows of information.

Prince 2 offers a process-based approach to key areas of project management. It is made up of eight high-level processes:

- directing a project (DP);
- planning (PL);
- starting up a project (SU);
- initiating a project (IP);
- controlling a stage (CS);
- managing product delivery (MP);
- managing stage boundaries (SB);

■ closing a project (CP).

UML

The Unified Modelling Language (UML) is a non-proprietary, object modelling and specification language used in software engineering. The UML model can be used to showcase the functionality of a system, the structure and sub-structure, and the internal behaviour. The following are artefacts that can be created using UML:

■ use cases
■ class diagrams
■ sequence diagrams
■ state activity diagrams.

RAD

Rapid Application Development (RAD) is a software development process that involves iterative development and the construction of prototypes.

Core Elements of RAD

RAD has six core elements:

■ prototyping
■ iterative development
■ timeboxing
■ team members
■ management approach
■ RAD tools.

Agile

Agile software development is a conceptual framework for undertaking software engineering projects. Agile methods attempt to minimise risk by developing software in short timeboxes, called iterations, which typically last one to four weeks. Each iteration is like a miniature software project of its own and includes all of the tasks necessary to release the mini-increment of new functionality: planning, requirements analysis, design, coding, testing and documentation. While iteration may not add enough functionality to warrant releasing the product, an agile software project intends to be capable of releasing new software at the end of every iteration. At the end of each iteration, the team re-evaluates project priorities.

Extreme Programming

Extreme Programming (XP) is a software engineering methodology for the development of software projects. It prescribes a set of day-to-day practices for developers and managers; the practices are meant to embody and encourage particular values and:

■ involve new or prototype technology, where the requirements change rapidly, or some development is required to discover unforeseen implementation problems;

■ are small and more easily managed though informal methods.

Pair Programming

Pair programming involves having two programmers working side by side, collaborating on the same design, algorithm, code or test. One programmer, the driver, has control of the keyboard/mouse and actively implements the program. The other programmer, the observer, continuously observes the work of the driver to identify tactical (syntactic, spelling, etc.) defects and also thinks strategically about the direction of the work. On demand, the two programmers can brainstorm any challenging problem. Because the two programmers periodically switch roles, they work together as equals to develop software.

Business and Systems Analysis Methods

Business and systems analysis methods adopted in the development of software in the investment management industry are vast and varied but the following are the most commonly used.

Business rules approach

The business rules approach is a development methodology where rules are in a form that is used by but not embedded in business process management systems.

The business rules approach formalises an enterprise's critical business rules in a language the manager and technologist can understand. Business rules create an unambiguous statement of what a business does, with information to decide on a proposition. The formal specification becomes information for process and rules engines to run.

Entity-relationship diagrams

The entity-relationship model or entity-relationship diagram (ERD) is a data model or diagram for high-level descriptions of conceptual data models and it provides a graphical notation for representing such data models in the form of entity-relationship diagrams. Such models are typically used in the first stage of information system design; they are used, for example, to describe information needs and/or the type of information that is to be stored in the database during the requirements analysis.

Prototyping

The prototyping model is a software development process that begins with requirements collection, followed by prototyping and user evaluation. Often the end users may not be able to provide a complete set of application objectives, detailed input, processing or output requirements in the initial stage. After the user evaluation, another prototype will be built based on feedback from users and again the cycle returns to customer evaluation. The cycle starts by listening to the user, followed by building or revising a mock-up and letting the user test the mock-up, then it goes back to the beginning again.

Testing Methods

The following are common testing methods adopted in systems development in investment management.

Equivalence Partitioning

Equivalence partitioning is a systematic process that identifies, on the basis of whatever information is available, a set of classes of input conditions to be tested. Each class is a representative of a large set of other possible tests.

Boundary Value Analysis

Boundary value analysis is a variant and refinement of equivalence partitioning with two major differences. First, rather than selecting any element in an equivalence class as being representative, elements are selected such that each edge of the equivalence class is the subject of a test.

Second, rather than focusing exclusively on input conditions, output conditions are also explored by defining output equivalent classes.

Error Guessing

Error guessing is an ad hoc approach, based on intuition and experience, to identifying tests that are considered likely to expose errors. The basic approach is to make a list of possible errors or error-prone situations and then develop tests based on the list.

Tools

Some of the most popular tools used in the investment management industry for software development, project management, test management and defect tracking are as follows.

IBM Rational Rose

Rational Rose is an object-oriented, Unified Modelling Language (UML) software design tool intended for the visual modelling and component construction of enterprise-level software applications.

IBM Rational ClearCase

ClearCase provides life-cycle management and control of software development assets. It is used in investment management firms for change management and control of source code and artefacts.

Mercury QTP

This Mercury interactive test automation tool is used mainly in investment management firms for the automation of regression tests and data-driven tests.

IBM Rational ClearQuest

ClearQuest helps to automate and enforce development processes, manage issues throughout the project life cycle and facilitate communication between all stakeholders across the enterprise software. It is used in investment management firms for defect management and change tracking.

Mercury Test Director (Quality Centre)

This Mercury interactive test management tool is used in investment management firms for storing requirements, test cases and scripts. Test Director is fast becoming the industry standard for test management.

Oracle Designer

Oracle Designer offers a toolset to model, generate and capture the requirements and design of web-based applications quickly, accurately and efficiently, and also to assess the impact of changing those designs and applications.

PowerDesigner

PowerDesigner is a business process modelling approach to aligning business and IT, is an enterprise data modelling and database design solution that helps implement effective Enterprise Architecture and brings a powerful conceptual data model to the application development life cycle.

PowerDesigner uniquely combines several standard data modelling techniques (UML, Business Process Modelling and market-leading data modelling) together with leading development environments such as .NET, Workspace, PowerBuilder, Java, Eclipse, etc. to bring business analysis and formal database design solutions to the traditional software development life cycle. It also works with all modern RDBMSs.

Common IT Skills Required

IT professionals usually update their skills in line with technological advancements but to compete in the skills market in investment management, some specific skills are required in various capacities. These are some of the skills that employers in the industry demand:

- **JAVA** – experience and knowledge of Java Collections Classes, threads, swing development, design patterns, messaging middleware concepts.
- **C++** – experience and knowledge of C++ multi-threading, STL, design patterns, messaging middleware concepts.
- **BizTalk** – good knowledge of Microsoft BizTalk.
- **ControlM** – knowledge and experience of ControlM – a system that pro-

vides advanced production-scheduling capabilities across the enterprise from a single point of control – is desirable.

- ▓ **.NET** – experience and understanding of Web services – small, reusable applications that help computers from many different operating-system platforms work together by exchanging messages – from technical and business perspectives.
- ▓ **J2EE (Java 2 Platform, Enterprise Edition)** – appreciation and experience of this platform is essential.
- ▓ **Junit** – knowledge of Junit – a regression-testing framework used by the developer who implements unit tests in Java – is desirable.
- ▓ **Market Data** – ability to interpret the data feeds from providers like Reuters and Bloomberg.
- ▓ **XP** – proficiency in Microsoft XP is important.
- ▓ **Microsoft Excel** – it is essential to be proficient in Microsoft Excel. It is also desirable to have good skills in VBA.
- ▓ **Business Objects** – knowledge of Business Objects and the ability to manipulate data for reports in Business Objects is an essential skill to have.
- ▓ **UNIX** – it is essential to have knowledge and experience of UNIX and Linux and associated scripting languages.
- ▓ **SQL** – proficiency in writing SQL queries. Most investment management firms use Sybase and Oracle databases; therefore it is vital to have a good command of PL/SQL and also TransactSQL, and tools such as TOAD and Oracle Discoverer.
- ▓ **IBM Websphere** – the ability to perform administrative tasks such as starting and stopping processes and deploying builds in IBM Websphere is essential.
- ▓ **Messaging platforms** – knowledge of IBM's MQ series, MINT, Tuxedo and Rendezvous ETX is desirable.
- ▓ **Cruise Control** – knowledge of Cruise Control is desirable. Cruise Control is usually used for deploying software builds.
- ▓ **FIX protocol** – at least a basic knowledge of FIX (Financial Information Exchange) protocol is desirable.
- ▓ **XML** – a rudimentary knowledge of XML is required to work successfully in IT in investment management. Knowledge of the structure of XML messages is important, especially the financial variants such as FpML and FIXML.
- ▓ **SWIFT** – understanding the format and categories of SWIFT messages is essential.
- ▓ **TIBCO** – good knowledge of TIBCO business process and optimisation software is desirable.
- ▓ **ISO 15022** – knowledge of ISO15022 – principles necessary to provide the different communities of users with the tools to design message types to support their specific information flows – is important. It is necessary to understand the set of syntax and message design rules and the dictionary of data fields.

Soft Skills

- **Numeracy** – having numerical skills is important if readers want to work on banking projects as there are usually complex calculations involved in developing and verifying the functionality of some applications.
- **Business acumen** – a solid business acumen and awareness is required to perform well in the investment management sector. Readers should make a habit of reading news in the financial pages of the broadsheets or periodicals such as The Economist and Bloomberg Markets, and watching programmes on Bloomberg Television and CNBC's squawk box.
- **Good communication skills** – it is essential to be able to explain concepts in banking and finance from both a technical and business standpoint in order to gain the confidence of the business users.
- **Business analysis skills** – the ability to understand business requirements and be able to document them is a nice skill to have. Readers should learn the art of extracting vital information from workshops and meetings with business users.
- **Project management skills** – project management skills are essential, especially in the appreciation of Information Technology Infrastructure Library – a framework of best practice approaches intended to facilitate the delivery of high-quality information technology (IT) services. This is increasingly important with the advent of outsourcing.
- **Inductive thinking** – the ability to think inductively will stand readers in good stead.
- **Good writing skills** – good writing skills are important in order to produce high-quality documentation.
- **Ability to withstand pressure** – the work environment in the banking sector is highly pressurised and as such requires the ability to withstand pressure.
- **Ability to see the "big picture"** – ability to see the bigger picture in order to understand the wider implications of the work tasks for the profitability of organisations.
- **Basic understanding of economics** – a basic understanding of economics is required to work in the sector if readers want a fulfilling career in investment management.
- **Proficiency in different languages** – a proficiency in different languages would be beneficial as some of the projects could span different continents. The discerning IT professional should be able to communicate with business users and other IT professionals in another language.
- **Negotiation skills** – good negotiation skills are important because of the aggressive deadlines to which projects are executed.

The Future

This chapter covers the future trends that might shape business and IT in investment management.

The Future: What does it hold for Investment Management in Business and IT?

Investment management firms are faced with a future that requires radical changes in an increasingly global, technology-enabled and heavily regulated subsector of the financial sector in order to remain competitive. With continuing pricing pressure on passive and traditional actively managed products threatening revenue growth, and demands of both institutional and retail investors changing more than in the past, investment managers that don't react quickly will be left by the wayside.

The way that investments are managed will fundamentally change in the coming decades. The changes will unfold as investors and managers seek out portfolio structures that maximise the likelihood of meeting investment objectives.

Investment management firms will be looking into the future, concentrating on the following key areas of IT and business:

- Globalisation and consolidation;
- Promotion of Compliance;
- Product Innovation;
- Role of Custodians in Investment Management;
- Consolidation of Islamic Asset Management;
- Outsourcing to New Labour Markets;
- Post MiFID IT Challenges;
- Better Operational Risk Control.

Globalisation and Consolidation

The drivers for growth for investment management firms in the years ahead are consolidation and exploitation of new markets, especially China and India, to accomplish the quest for globalisation. The other BRIC countries, namely Brazil and Russia, will also offer opportunities for these firms in the near future.

According to Delloitte, China is ahead of the pack in terms of opportunities. As of December 2005, 20 foreign fund managers had moved in.[49] This is on the back of demand for investment products and financial advice from the China's burgeoning middle class. However, not all the new entrants have achieved their primary objective of profitability in this country; it has proved to be elusive. Industry experts are of the opinion that a long-term view is required to succeed in the Chinese market.

Notable examples of investment management firms that have made substantial commitments in China, albeit with little success, are ING of the Netherlands and Schroeder of the UK. These companies made incursions in the market through joint ventures and made substantial losses in the last quarter of

49 A Bumpy ride in China, James Walker, Wall Street Journal, March 1 2006.

2005.[50] Other investment management companies are adopting a more restrained investment strategy until they can chart a course to profitability.

As for India, the interest in this market from foreign institutions is evident owing to the rapid economic growth, strong equity market, declining interest rate and easing of protectionist regulations. Mutual fund assets under management almost doubled between 2003 and 2006 to $48 million, while the Bombay Stock Exchange's Sensex index tripled during the same period. About half of the money is managed by non-Indian[51] companies, for example Fidelity which started its first domestic mutual fund in 2005.

Promotion of Compliance

Global investment management firms are under increasing pressure to promote compliance within their organisations as it is deemed critical to their firm's reputation and ultimately to their ability to grow and prosper. Firms operating in Asia find that compliance can be difficult in this region, where rules differ and sometimes are in conflict with one another from country to country.

According to Delloitte, in Japan regulators demand that each subsidiary and affiliate of a foreign firm must have its own local compliance department or compliance officer, with local control.[52] This approach may make it difficult to achieve economies of scale.

Investment management firms will be looking to have input into the investment management rules in the foreign markets in which they have interests, as in the case of Japan where these rules are yet to be harmonised. The promising markets of China and India are also still developing and/or modifying their regulations and this approach could likely be the most plausible.

Product Innovation

Among the top priorities for investment managers in the near future is product innovation in the form of variety of product ranging from alternative institutional portfolio strategies – portable alpha and liability-driven investment (LDI) and hedge funds – to hedge-like mutual funds. ETFs will continue to multiply and offer exposure to new types of assets.

Investment management firms will lay emphasis on innovative products across the asset classes that are not in the market as yet with a view to increasing their revenue streams and generating better alpha for their clients. Innovative products that may be become popular in future include life-cycle funds in the UK and US and both private and public real-estate investment vehicles with assets in China, Korea, Singapore and other fast-growing Asia-Pacific markets.

50 Huge losses for Chinese Joint Ventures, January 23 2006.
51 Mutual-Fund Hot Spot: India, Shefali Anand, Wall Street Journal, March 10, 2006.
52 Compliance Function at Market Intermediaries Final Report, Technical Committee of the International Organisation of Securities Commissions, March 2006.

In order to achieve continuous product innovation, investment management firms will also need to attract skilled investment managers and quants.

Role of Custodians in Investment Management

With the growing importance and volumes of Over the Counter (OTC) derivatives, custodians need to strengthen their infrastructure for handling the settlement of the traded products.

Custodians will be building technology infrastructures and message capabilities to receive electronic messages from their investment management clients. They will be improving their service levels by adopting accepted Financial Products Mark-up Language (FpML) messaging standards and building a seamless interface with third-party information providers to provide them with a competitive edge. They will be building interfaces with their clients' back-office processes to bridge the gap in straight-through processing.

Consolidation of Islamic Asset Management

Islamic asset managers will be more in the mainstream in the years to come and the convergence between Islamic and conventional asset management will be more evident. The Islamic sector, which is now the most dynamic in international finance and already estimated to be controlling around $500 billion in assets, is expected to grow and asset management will be the cornerstone of the growth.

Western financial institutions are already opening "Islamic windows" or fully fledged Islamic financing units. According to Moody's Investor Services, some $200 billion of assets lie in these Islamic windows in the Middle East. Financial institutions such as UBS are known to have set up an Islamic window in asset management.

It is expected that in the future, Shari'a-compliant financial institutions will be set up in Western countries, a trend which started when the FSA in the UK awarded a licence for the first dedicated Shari'a-compliant investment bank, European Islamic Investment Bank (EIIB). The licence award also confirms London's emerging reputation as the main Western centre for Islamic finance.

Outsourcing to New Labour Markets

IT service providers in cheaper labour markets such as India are building software platforms that furnish every business process needed and secure all regulatory approvals. The dexterity of these IT service providers is attracting global players in investment management to increasingly outsource their IT requirements to these companies.

This trend will continue well into the future as cost savings provide a strategic competitive advantage for the firms that go down this route. Outsourcing to emerging labour markets, for example Russia, will be the norm. Russia has been one of the hottest labour markets for the outsourcing of IT in recent times. While opinions have been polarised about Russian IT and software development capabilities, the strengths of this market in this regard cannot be called into question. According to Gartner[53] group, in 2007 Russia will have captured a 5% market share of the offshore services revenue of North America and Western Europe.

Post MiFID IT Challenges

With the advent of the introduction of MiFID, investment management firms are gearing up on the technology front, but it is post-MiFID when there will be technological challenges that they will be faced with in future. It has been widely published that exchanges such as Deutsche Borse and Swiss Exchange are committing themselves to huge investments in their systems to address specific requirements of the directive. To this end, investment management companies will need radical changes in their IT systems to take advantage of the various initiatives in the pipeline at these exchanges.

Investment managers will need to come up with innovative algorithms as algorithmic trading will receive a boost in the post-MiFID era. There will be more pressing needs for this when buy side clients seek to combine trading strategies, such as crossing, and require a broader range of algorithms to base these strategies on.

Better Operational Risk Control

Investment management firms are discovering that operational risk is getting increasingly important and more important to control. There is an explosion in trade and transaction values with the advent of globalisation and rapid innovation has resulted in the production of increasingly complex financial products and trading activities. To this end, operational risk control solutions that are capable of dynamically adapting to new situations, integrating data from disparate silos and feeds, are being adopted/deployed. The aim is to create an enterprise-wide view of the risks the organisation is facing.

The key, in future, for effective operational risk control will be the management of data as a key enterprise asset. The solutions that will be deployed will have the ability to extract data from any source, manipulate the data into a form that is best suited for analysis and processing and deliver that data to any destination in a prescribed format.

Conclusion

IT professionals that aspire to a career in investment management will embrace all the factors discussed above in order to get them prepared for the hybrid role – IT/business savvy professional – that will the norm in the future.

---

53 Gartner Inc. "Russia is Building Its Offshore Services Credibility", Joseph Feiman and Ian Marriot. October 2004.

Appendix

Sector Classifications[54]

Funds principally targeting income – Immediate Income

▪ **UK Gilts** – Funds which invest at least 95% of their assets in Sterling-denominated (or hedged back to Sterling), Triple AAA rated, government-backed securities, with at least 75% invested in UK government securities (Gilts).

▪ **UK Index-Linked Gilts** – Funds which invest at least 90% of their assets in UK Index-Linked Government securities (Gilts).

▪ **UK Corporate Bond** – Funds which invest at least 80% of their assets in Sterling-denominated (or hedged back to Sterling), Triple BBB minus or above bonds (as measured by Standard & Poor's or an equivalent external rating agency – Moody's Baa or above). This excludes convertibles.

▪ **UK Other Bond** – Funds investing at least 80% of their assets in Sterling-denominated (or hedged back to Sterling) securities, and at least 20% of their assets in below BBB minus bonds (as measured by Standard and Poor's or an equivalent external rating agency), convertibles and income-producing preference shares.

▪ **Global Bonds** – Funds which invest at least 80% of their assets in fixed-interest stocks. All funds which contain more than 80% fixed-interest investments are to be classified under this heading regardless of the fact that they may have more than 80% in a particular geographic sector, unless that geographic area is the UK, when the fund should be classified under the relevant UK heading.

▪ **UK Equity & Bond Income** – Funds which invest at least 80% of their assets in the UK, between 20% and 80% in UK fixed-interest securities and between 20% and 80% in UK equities. These funds aim to have a yield of 120% or above of the FT All Share Index.

Funds principally targeting income – Growing Income

▪ **UK Equity Income** – Funds which invest at least 80% of their assets in UK equities and which aim to achieve a yield on the underlying portfolio in excess of 110% of the FTSE All Share yield (net of tax). The distributable income may differ from the yield quoted in financial publications.

Funds principally targeting capital – Capital Growth/Total Return

▪ **UK Zeros** – Funds investing at least 80% of their assets in Sterling-denominated (or hedged back to Sterling) securities, and at least 80% of their assets in zero dividend preference shares or equivalent instruments (i.e. not income producing). This excludes preference shares which produce an income.

▪ **UK All Companies** – Funds which invest at least 80% of their assets in UK equities which have a primary objective of achieving capital growth.

54 Source : Investment Management Association.

- **UK Smaller Companies** – Funds which invest at least 80% of their assets in UK equities of companies which form the bottom 10% by market capitalisation.
- **Japan** – Funds which invest at least 80% of their assets in Japanese equities.
- **Japanese Smaller Companies** – Funds which invest at least 80% of their assets in Japanese equities of companies which form the bottom 30% by market capitalisation.
- **Asia Pacific including Japan** – Funds which invest at least 80% of their assets in Asia Pacific equities including a Japanese content. The Japanese content must make up less than 80% of assets.
- **Asia Pacific excluding Japan** – Funds which invest at least 80% of their assets in Asia Pacific equities and exclude Japanese securities.
- **North America** – Funds which invest at least 80% of their assets in North American equities.
- **North American Smaller Companies** – Funds which invest a least 80% of their assets in North American equities of companies which form the bottom 20% by market capitalisation.
- **Europe including UK** – Funds which invest at least 80% of their assets in European equities. They may include UK equities, but these must not exceed 80% of the funds' assets.
- **Europe excluding UK** – Funds which invest at least 80% of their assets in European equities and exclude UK securities.
- **European Smaller Companies** – Funds which invest at least 80% of their assets in European equities of companies which form the bottom 20% by market capitalisation in the European market. They may include UK equities, but these must not exceed 80% or the funds' assets. ("Europe" includes all countries in the MSCI/FTSE pan-European indices.)
- **Cautious Managed** – Funds which offer investment in a range of assets, with the maximum equity exposure restricted to 60% of the fund and with at least 30% invested in fixed interest and cash. There is no specific requirement to hold a minimum percentage of non-UK equity. Assets must be at least 50% in Sterling/Euro and equities are deemed to include convertibles.
- **Balanced Managed** – Funds offer investment in a range of assets, with the maximum equity exposure restricted to 85% of the fund. At least 10% must be held in non-UK equities. Assets must be at least 50% in Sterling/Euro and equities are deemed to include convertibles.
- **Active Managed** – Funds offer investment in a range of assets, with the Manager being able to invest up to 100% in equities at their discretion. At least 10% must be held in non-UK equities. There is no minimum Sterling/Euro balance and equities are deemed to include convertibles. At any one time the asset allocation of these funds may hold a high proportion of non-equity assets such that the asset allocation would by default place the fund in either the Balanced or Cautious sector. These funds would remain in this sector on these occasions since it is the Manager's stated intention to retain the right to invest up to 100% in equities.

■ **Global Growth** – Funds which invest at least 80% of their assets in equities (but not more than 80% in UK assets) and which have the prime objective of achieving growth of capital.

■ **Global Emerging Markets** – Funds which invest 80% or more of their assets directly or indirectly in emerging markets as defined by the World Bank, without geographical restriction. Indirect investment, e.g. China shares listed in Hong Kong, should not exceed 50% of the portfolio.

Note: The above sectors also require funds to be broadly diversified within the relevant country/region/asset class. Funds that concentrate solely on a specialist theme, sector or single market size (or a single country in a multi-currency region) would be incorporated in the Specialist sector (see below), or in the case of tech funds, in the Technology & Telecommunications sector.

Funds principally targeting capital protection

■ **Money Market** – Funds which invest at least 95% of their assets in money market instruments (i.e. cash and near cash, such as bank deposits, certificates of deposit, very short-term fixed-interest securities or floating-rate notes).

■ **Protected/Guaranteed Funds** – Funds, other than money market funds, which principally aim to provide a return of a set amount of capital back to the investor (either explicitly guaranteed or via an investment strategy highly likely to achieve this objective) plus some market upside.

Specialist Sectors

■ **Specialist** – Funds that have an investment universe that is not accommodated by the mainstream sectors. Performance ranking of funds within the sector as a whole is inappropriate, given the diverse nature of its constituents.

■ **Technology & Telecommunications** – Funds which invest at least 80% of their assets in technology and telecommunications sectors as defined by major index providers.

■ **Personal Pensions** – Funds which are only available for use in a personal pension plan or FSAVC scheme.

Present arrangements for unit-trust personal pension schemes require providers to set up a separate personal pension unit trust under an overall tax-sheltered umbrella. These funds then, in turn, invest in the group's equivalent mainstream trusts. Pension funds are not to be confused with "Exempt" funds which are flagged separately.

Note: In the gilt/bond sectors, a security with 0–3 months to maturity will be treated as cash. Securities maturing within 3–12 months will be treated as bonds. In the Managed sectors (Cautious Managed, Balanced Managed, Active Managed and UK Equity and Bond), cash and fixed income will be treated as interchangeable.

Specialist Recruitment Agencies

Robert Half	www.roberthalf.co.uk
Michael Page	www.michaelpage.com
McGregor Boyall	www.mcgregor-boyall.com
Badenoch and Clark	www.badenochandclark.com
Robert Walters	www.robertwalters.com
Madison Black	www.madisonblack.com
Aston Carter	www.astoncarter.co.uk
Morgan Hutchins Associates	www.morganhutchins.com
Highams Recruitment	www.hatstand-ltd.com
Hudson	www.hudson.com
Lorien	www.lorien.co.uk
Modis	www.752Solutions.com
Cititec	www.cititec.com
Real Resourcing	www.realresourcing.com/
Anson McCade	www.ansonmccade.com
Penta Consulting	www.pentaconsulting.com
Joslin Rowe	www.joslinrowe.com
JM Contracts	www.jmpeople.com
Adlam Consulting	www.adlam.cocm
Project Partners	www.projpartners.com
33-6 Consultancy	www.33-6.com

Bibliography

130/30 Portfolios set to come to the fore in 2007, available from: www.citywire.co.uk

About Bank of England, available from www.bankofengland.co.uk/about/more_about

About CESR, available from www.cesr-eu.org

Allianz Annual Report 2006, available from www.allianz.com/en/allianz_group/investor_relations/

Apprenticed Investor: Six Keys to Stock Selection, available from www.thestreet.com

Barclays Annual Report 2006, available from www.investorrelations.barclays.co.uk/investor_relations

BearingPoint 'Enabling the holistic enterprise with web services and services-oriented architecture'. *Financial Services Technology*, Journal Vol. 1 Issue 1. pp 4–5.

Bentley, C. (1999) *Prince 2. A Practical Handbook.* Butterworth Heinemann.

Block, R. (2006) *Investing in REITs: Real Estate Investment Trusts.* Bloomberg Press.

Boutiques can be best of breed, available from www.efinancialnews.com/archive/keyword/boutique_fund_management

City Business Series (2006) *Fund Management.* International Financial Services.

Chisholm, C. (2002) *An Introduction to Capital Markets.* Wiley Finance.

Dark Liquidity Pools make a splash with US traders, available from www.efinancialnews.com

Deloitte Financial Services. (2006) *Global Asset Management Outlook: Integrating Strategy with Experience in a Changing World.*

Emerging Trading Technologies created serious value challenges for institutional brokerages, available from www.acccenture.com

European SRI, available from www.eiris.org

Essinger, J. and Lowe, D. (1997) *Handbook of Investment Management: The Definitive Guide for the Investment Professional.* Financial Times Prentice Hall.

Exchanges Boost Technology Systems, available from www.efinancialnews.com

Grinold, R. and Kahn, R. (1999) *Active Portfolio Management: A quantitative approach for producing superior returns and selecting superior money managers.* McGraw-Hill Publishing Co.

Gulf States to Continue Strong Economic Growth in 2007, available from www.menafn.com

Hughes, D. (2004) *Introduction to Asset Management*. Financial World Publishing.

Introduction to Exchange-Traded Funds, available from www.investopedia.com

Investment Management, available from http://en.wikipedia.org/wiki/Investment_management

Investment Management Association (2006) *Asset Management Survey*, available from www.ima.org

Jaffer, S. (2004) *Islamic Asset Management: forming the future for Shari'a compliant investment strategies*. Euromoney Books.

Kit, E. (1995) *Software Testing in the Real World*. Addison-Wesley.

Learn About Service Oriented Architecture (SOA), available from www.microsoft.com/biztalk/solutions/soa/overview

Litterman, B. (2003) *Modern Investment Management: An Equilibrium Approach*. John Wiley & Sons Inc.

Loader, D. (2006) *Fundamentals of Fund Administration*. Butterworth-Heinemann.

Lofthouse, S. (2000) *Investment Management*. John Wiley and Sons.

London: dynamic and exciting with a dark side, available from www.telegraph.co.uk

Merrill Lynch 'ML FX Clone' Model Replicate Hedge Fund FX Strategies, available from www.thetradenews.com

Michaud, R. (1998) *Efficient Asset Management: A Practical Guide to Stock Portfolio Optimization and Asset Allocation*. Oxford University Press Inc.

One Company – Three Brands, available from www.indexco.com

ProfitStars (2006) Operational Risk Management and Control: *Managing Data as a Key Enterprise Asset*, available from www.ManageForPerformance.com

Property Derivatives: an Overview, available from www.financialsense.com/fsu/editorials/shvartsman/2005/0929

Russell, R. (2006) *An Introduction to Fund Management*. Wiley Finance.

Satchell, S. and Scowcroft, A. (2003) *Advances in Portfolio Construction and Implementation*. Butterworth-Heinemann Ltd.

Schneider, G. and Winter, J. (1998) *Applying Use Cases*. Addison-Wesley.

Schoenfeld, S. (2004) *Active Index Investing: Maximizing Portfolio Performance and Minimizing Risk through Global Index Strategies.* John Wiley & Sons Inc.

S&P Fund Management Rating, available from www.funds.morningstar.com/

SRI Strategies, available from www.eiris.org

State Street Annual Report 2006, available from http://phx.corporate-ir.net/phoenix.zhtml?c=78261&p=irol-IRHome

Swiss Derivatives Review (2004) *Currency – an Asset Class.*

Tata Consultancy Services (2005) *Role of Custodians in OTC Derivatives – A Critical Analysis.*

The Sunday Times Magazine (2006) *How London Topped New York.*

UBS Annual Report 2006, available from www.ubs.com/1/e/investors/topics.html

Index

Index compiled by Lynette Davidson

Other Titles in the Bizle Professional Series

Business Knowledge for IT in
Global Investment Banking

Business Knowledge for IT in
Prime Brokerage

Business Knowledge for IT
in Private Equity

Business Knowledge for IT in
Retail Banking

Business Knowledge for IT in
Hedge Funds

Business Knowledge for IT in
Private Wealth

**These and other exciting titles can be pre-ordered from
Amazon sites worldwide or from www.essvale.com**

Printed in the United Kingdom
by Lightning Source UK Ltd.
128462UK00001B/99-118/A